G000098779

Green Devils

Green Devils

THE IRISH AND MANCHESTER UNITED

KEITH FALKINER

HACHETTE
BOOKS
IRELAND

First published in 2008 by Hachette Books Ireland
A division of Hachette Livre UK Ltd

Copyright © Keith Falkiner 2008

1

The right of Keith Falkiner to be identified as the Author of the Work has been asserted by him in accordance with the Copyright, Designs and Patents Act, 1988.

All rights reserved. No part of this publication may be reproduced, stored in a retrieval system, or transmitted, in any form or by any means without the prior written permission of the publisher, nor be otherwise circulated in any form of binding or cover other than that in which it is published and without a similar condition being imposed on the subsequent purchaser.

A CIP catalogue record for this title is available from the British Library.

ISBN 978-0-340-96029-5

Typeset in Garamond
Cover and text design by Anú Design, Tara
Printed and bound in Italy by L.E.G.O. SpA - Vicenza

Hodder Headline Ireland's policy is to use papers that are natural, renewable and recyclable products and made from wood grown in sustainable forests. The logging and manufacturing processes are expected to conform to the environmental regulations of the country of origin.

Hachette Books Ireland
8 Castlecourt Centre
Castleknock
Dublin 15
Ireland

A division of Hachette Livre, 338 Euston Road, London NW1 3BH, England

Contents

Introduction

It all started with the late nineteenth century signing of a pacey County Antrim forward.

The year was 1893 and the name Manchester United hadn't even come into football reckoning.

Newton Heath – a tiny club situated in the northwest of England was still making its first tentative steps into the world of professional football and the club's ambitions were little more than maintaining its new-found status within the Football League's First Division.

Newton Heath may have ultimately failed in this modest objective, but the club's signing of Linfield forward John Peden was the beginning of something that would prove much more significant in the history of Manchester United Football Club. It fostered an early connection between Ireland and the Manchester club that is now unbreakable.

It was a connection which grew even stronger after Newton Heath changed its name to Manchester United in 1902, as heaps of young stars crossed the Irish Sea to begin their new lives as footballers for one of the world's most famous clubs.

As early as 1914, Manchester United had its first Irish captain in the shape of Dublin-born half-back Patrick O'Connell.

O'Connell's stint as captain may have only lasted a year, but Irish-born leaders of Manchester United later became a feature in some of the club's most glorious periods.

Legendary Dubliner Johnny Carey kick-started the trend when he triumphantly held the FA Cup aloft as the proud captain of Manchester United in 1948.

Four years later, Carey became the first Irishman to captain an English team to both the FA Cup and First Division title as Manchester United were transformed into football powerhouses under Scottish manager Sir Matt Busby.

Busby's love of the Irish never ceased in his almost quarter of a century reign as Manchester United manager, as he signed many a great player from these shores to play in the club's famous red shirts.

And such was the flamboyant style of Busby's teams that football lovers in Ireland began to support Manchester United in their droves.

The Irish fans' lover affair with the club started in earnest in the late 1940s but had reached massive levels by the time the renowned 'Busby Babes' came to Dublin for a European Cup encounter in 1957.

The tragic events of the Munich Air Disaster in February 1958, when eight United players including Dublin-born Liam Whelan were killed, only served to strengthen the ties between the club and this country.

Manchester United's stern resolve not to buckle under such a traumatic tragedy increased the club's popularity in Ireland – and the 1960s became one of the best ever decades for Irish United players.

Dedicated Cork full-back Noel Cantwell followed in the footsteps of Johnny Carey as he led United to the FA Cup in 1963.

But Cantwell's successful captaincy was soon outshone by the brilliant feats of young Belfast winger George Best.

A player of amazing pace and panache, Best's stunning natural talent and sparkling personality made him a hero all Irish fans could be proud of.

The fans were prouder still when a Best-inspired United captured not only two English league titles in three years but added a European Cup in 1968.

Sadly this proved to be the pinnacle of Best's time at United, but as the East Belfast star's powers began to wane in the mid-1970s, a new bunch of Irish heroes emerged.

Tenacious forward Sammy McIlroy maintained Belfast's proud Man Utd tradition throughout the 1970s, whilst teen sensation Norman Whiteside continued it through the 1980s.

During the 1970s and 1980s, United didn't find much league success, but a bevy of Irish players from Jimmy Nichol to Paul McGrath, Kevin Moran and Frank Stapleton helped the club to some wonderful Wembley moments in the FA Cup.

When United returned to the pinnacle of the English game in the 1990s, Ireland's presence at the club was as prominent as ever.

Loyal Cork servant Denis Irwin amassed no less than thirteen major titles, whilst fellow Corkman Roy Keane became United's most decorated captain of all time by his retirement in 2005.

Ireland's influence on the history of Manchester United really can't be underestimated.

While it can be said for certain that Scotland has produced the club's two greatest managers, it is equally true to say that Ireland has provided possibly United's greatest player in Best and its greatest captain in Keane.

Far from being on the periphery of Manchester United's tremendous success over the past century, Irishmen have been central to the club's achievements. Without their presence, Manchester United might not have become the club it is today.

Keith Falkiner
September 2008

Acknowledgements

A big thank you to Neil Fetherstonhaugh, Claire Rourke, Ciara Doorley, Cathal McMahon, Maeve Donlon, Teresa Van Martens, Eddie Gibbons, Trevor McLave, the National Library of Ireland, my dad Noel Falkiner, Tina Falkiner, my partner Yvonne McWeeney and my daughter Aoibheann for helping me put this book together.

Keith Falkiner, September 2008

This book is dedicated to
double Special Olympics gold medallist
Derek Kelly;
a real Man Utd fan and a true inspiration.

Newton Heath

(1878-1902)

Thousands of Irish devotees who make the pilgrimage to the hollowed turf of Old Trafford each year, but the grandiose surrounds of Manchester United's fabulous 'Theatre of Dreams' couldn't be further from the club's humble beginnings as a football team for local railway workers.

The all-conquering Manchester United that we know today began life in 1878 under the name Newton Heath. The club was formed as the works team of the Lancashire and Yorkshire Railway depot and played their home games on a small, run-down pitch on North Road in Manchester.

Sporting shirts that were half green and half gold, Newton Heath's first few seasons as an amateur football team proved very successful. They made it to five successive finals of the Manchester and District Cup in the 1880s, which prompted the club to attempt to turn professional in 1885.

Despite failing to gain entry into the expanding English Football League that year, Newton Heath – who had picked up the moniker the 'Heathens' – eventually joined the professional game in the Football Alliance League in 1889. Although not officially affiliated to the Football League, the Alliance acted like its Second Division.

During their first season in the Alliance, Newton Heath finished a respectable eighth out of twelve teams, winning nine of the twenty-two games they played.

Forwards John (Jack) Doughty and Edward Wilson and midfielder William Stewart were three of Newton Heath's star players that season, scoring the vast majority of the thirty league goals the team notched up.

Newton Heath consolidated their position in the professional game by finishing ninth in their second season in the Alliance.

Things looked up for the club the following season, when they acquired the deadly striking

The Heathens, 10 September 1892. The Newton Heath team that played in the first Football League game in Manchester. Robert Donaldson is third from the left in the front row.

skills of the club's first real top-notch sharp shooter in the form of Robert Donaldson.

Newton Heath had signed Donaldson in 1892 from Blackburn Rovers, who were one of the leading clubs in the English Football League at the time, and he immediately showed his class by scoring in his first game for Newton Heath, following on with five more goals in his next six games. Two hat-tricks in successive weeks followed for Donaldson against Lincoln City and Walsall respectively, as Newton Heath made a determined charge for the Alliance title.

The club eventually had to settle for second place behind winners Nottingham Forest, but their efforts that year gained them entry into the English Football League's First Division, after the Football Alliance disbanded and became an official Second Division.

Life in the First Division was hard for Newton Heath in their first year and they lost their first seven games on the trot. The whole season proved a struggle.

The club failed to win a single game away from their North Road home ground and finished bottom of the league. They were only saved from relegation through a play-off victory over Small Heath (now Birmingham City), who had been the runaway winners of the Second Division.

During that first season in the First

Division, Newton Heath had continued to play their matches at the small ground in North Road. However, visiting teams didn't like to play there as the pitch was a swamp and the dressing rooms were located half a mile away from the ground. Following complaints from rival clubs, Newton Heath began the 1893–94 season in a new ground across town in Bank Street, Clayton.

That season Newton Heath also signed a new forward in the shape of Linfield hotshot John Peden, who became the first man to make the move across the Irish Sea to the Manchester club. Peden got the chance to play in the club's new ground at Bank Street, which was larger and had more capacity for spectators, but it didn't bring the Heathens any new luck.

The club finished bottom of the First Division again, winning only six games all season, and they came up against Second Division winners Liverpool in a play-off contest. In a match played at Blackburn in front of 6,000 fans, Newton Heath lost 2–0 and were relegated to the Second Division, where they would remain for the next twelve years.

Despite moving to their new ground at Bank Street, the club continued to receive flak from visiting teams, particularly about the state of the pitch. After a league game against Walsall in March 1895, which Newton Heath had amazingly won 14–0, the Football League cancelled the result following complaints from the visiting team that the pitch was unplayable. The match had to be replayed a week later, after Newton Heath had set to

work at fixing up the pitch – they won again, though this time the margin was only 9–0.

Newton Heath finished their first season in the Second Division in third place but did not gain promotion back into the First Division. The club's best season in the Second Division came in 1896–97, when they finished runners up to Notts County.

The second-place finish meant the Heathens were involved in a mini-league for promotion with Notts County and the First Division's two bottom teams Sunderland and Burnley.

More than 18,000 fans turned up at Bank Street for Newton Heath's home game against Sunderland, which finished in a 1–1 draw.

Unfortunately, the Heathens lost the return leg at Roker Park and, following defeat away to Notts County, they failed to gain promotion that year. It was the same in 1898 and 1899, when Newton Heath came close both years, but never quite made it back into the First Division.

By the start of the new century, Newton Heath continued to languish in the shadow of their local rivals Manchester City, who played in the First Division.

The club had no English international players to speak of and had enjoyed just two years in the First Division, where they finished bottom of the league. With confidence in the team low, leading to poor attendances at games during the 1901–02 season, the club neared bankruptcy.

Dramatic action was needed to keep the club afloat and it duly arrived through an amazing twist of fate. After a four-day bazaar

John Henry Davies.

at Bank Street, which Newton Heath had held to raise money, the club captain Henry Stafford's St Bernard dog went missing and found his way into the hands of successful Manchester businessman John Henry Davies, who was managing director of Manchester Brewers.

Davies set about finding out who the dog's real owner was and came into contact with Stafford. After a meeting, Davies promised Stafford that he would plough money into Newton Heath. He led a group of business-men who invested £2,000 into the club and became its new president.

One of Davies' first duties at the club was to propose a change to the name Newton Heath – mainly because the club had not actually played at their Newton Heath location for over nine years. A number of names were given consideration, including Manchester Central and even Manchester Celtic. However, a young Italian immigrant by the name of Louis Rocca came up with the idea of renaming the club Manchester United. This new name met with widespread approval and, on 28 April 1902, Newton Heath became Manchester United.

The club also decided to ditch the team's old strip in favour of new red and white gear.

With this, a new football club, which would become famous the world over, was born.

Player Profiles

John Peden	
Place of birth:	Lisburn
Date of birth:	12 July 1863
Position:	Outside-left
Years at United:	1893–1894
	(Newton Heath)
Games played:	32
Goals:	8

Talented forward John Peden goes down in history as the first Irishman to move to the club that would become Manchester United, when he signed for Newton Heath in the summer of 1893.

A native of County Antrim, Peden was already an established Irish international player by the time he made the switch to England from his club Linfield, where he had been a founding member and where he had enjoyed an illustrious career, helping them to win three Irish League titles in a row.

He was thirty years old when he joined Newton Heath and slotted straight into their first team for the beginning of the 1893–94 season, when the club had just finished its first season in the English League's First Division.

Blessed with great natural pace, Peden could play equally well out wide on the wing or up front as a striker. His first game for the club came in a 3–2 win over Burnley at the

Heathen's home ground of Bank Street in September 1893.

Peden became a fixture in the first team that year, as his impressive displays, particularly on the wing, made him a popular player at the club. His first goals for Newton Heath came in a home win over West Brom, when he scored two of his team's four goals in a 4–1 victory. It was a rare bright moment for Newton

Heath, however, as they struggled badly that season.

Peden did manage to notch up another couple of goals against Aston Villa and Sheffield Wednesday but Newton Heath still lost both games during an awful seven game losing streak that dragged them to the foot of the table.

The club gained some relief with a 4–0 win over Middlesbrough in the FA Cup in January 1894 and Peden once again managed to get on the score sheet. However, they were soon brought back down to earth in a 5–0 hammering by Blackburn in a replay in the next round.

Peden added another two goals in Newton Heath's best performance that season as they beat Stoke City 6–2 at Bank Street in March 1895, but their inability to pick up points away from home kept them rooted in last spot. Those two goals proved to be Peden's last for the club, as he left for Sheffield Utd at the end of the season.

Peden's last game for Newton Heath came in a 2–0 play-off loss to Liverpool, which ensured their inevitable relegation from the First Division.

On the international front, Peden made his debut for Ireland in a 4–1 defeat to Scotland in February 1887. His international career spanned twelve years and the major highlight was scoring a hat-trick against Wales in a 4–3 win for Ireland in April 1893.

In his only season at Newton Heath, Peden scored eight goals in thirty-two appearances – a very respectable record by any player's standards.

Other Clubs: Linfield, Sheffield Utd, Distillery
International Record: Ireland
Caps: 24
Goals: 7

*United win the FA Cup for
the first time, 1909.*

The Early Manchester United Years

(1902-1945)

The first season for the team in red under its new name of Manchester United proved a relative success, considering the club had faced bankruptcy just a few months earlier. Playing in English football's second tier, United finished the 1902–03 season in fifth spot.

The club made one of its most significant moves in 1903 when it appointed the former Burnley manager Ernest Magnall as the team's first real manager. Magnall set about transforming Manchester United into one of the top teams in the country.

During his first full campaign in charge, United finished third in the Second Division, as his inspirational management style began to rub off on the players. Magnall brought in a number of new faces for the 1904–05 season – including former striker Jack Peddie from Plymouth Argyle and fellow forward Jack Allan – as United again finished third in the Second Division.

The club finally cracked promotion under Magnall's leadership the following year, and quickly became a real force in the First Division.

One of Magnall's first moves in the transfer market after United had gained promotion was to prove one of his most inspirational. He snapped up legendary winger Billy Meredith in October 1906 from local rivals Manchester City – a move that was to pay rich dividends for both player and club. Meredith was one of the best players of his generation and he soon helped United on their way to previously undreamed success.

In 1907, United finished their first season back in the top flight in eighth place but, just a year later, they were crowned the English First Division champions for the first time. It was a magnificent achievement for the club and they added to their success a year later by winning the FA Cup for the first time.

Magnall had created the first great Manchester United side and had laid the foundations for a footballing dynasty that has lasted a full century.

The condition of United's ground at Bank

Ernest Magnall. United's first manager.

Street still caused grave concern, however, and, in 1908, president John Davies decided he should help bankroll a new stadium for the club. A plot of land at Old Trafford was bought for £60,000 and plans for a 60,000-capacity stadium were made.

Designed by Scottish architect Archibald Leitch, the new ground featured under-cover seating in the south stand, while the remaining three stands were left as terraces and uncovered. Construction of the ground was swift and was completed by the end of 1909.

United played their first game at Old Trafford on 19 February 1910, losing 4–3 in a seven-goal thriller to Liverpool. However, the club quickly set about making Old Trafford a

fortress and claimed their second league title under Magnall's stewardship in 1911.

Although there had been no Irishmen at United to share in this joy, Magnall did sign a young Irish forward by the name of Mickey Hamill from Belfast Celtic in January 1911. Hamill only came in to the team at the start of the following season, when United could finish no better than a disappointing thirteenth.

Before the start of the 1912–13 season, Magnall made the controversial decision to leave United to manage Manchester City – to this day, he remains the only man to have managed both clubs. It was a move that caused shockwaves around Old Trafford, and his departure heralded a period of stagnation for the club. In fact, United didn't win another First Division title for forty years – the longest the club has ever gone without winning the league.

After Magnall left, former club chairman John Bentley took up the mantle of manager. Bentley, an ex-professional footballer himself, had been credited with playing a big part in the club's revival and subsequent move to Old Trafford. However, he was unable to transfer this success into management and United could only finish fourth and fourteenth in the league in the two years he was in charge.

When Bentley was relieved of his duties in 1914, he was replaced at the helm by former Middlesbrough manager Jack Robson. Robson had gained much success as a manager of both unfancied Middlesbrough and Crystal Palace but his time at United was severely interrupted by the outbreak of the First World War.

In May 1914, United had also brought in Dublin-born half-back Patrick O'Connell from Hull City. As one of the most accomplished defenders playing in the English League at the time, O'Connell became the first Irishman to captain United, after Robson named him the team's new leader.

During O'Connell's first – and only – season at the club, United finished way down in eighteenth place, after which the league was forced to take a break until 1919 because of the war.

When the First Division resumed, Robson led United to twelfth place in 1920.

The disturbance of the war had necessitated a massive influx of new players into the Old Trafford set-up and Robson never really had the time to develop a successful team.

United finished thirteenth in 1921 and, following the untimely death of Robson through pneumonia in January 1922, the club was relegated from the First Division by the end of that season.

John Chapman became United's new manager when they began life in the Second Division in the 1922–23 season. He drafted Northern Ireland forward Davy Lyner into the United squad from Glentoran but the Belfast man played only three games for the club throughout his time there.

Old Trafford, 1930. An aerial view of Old Trafford, showing the covered south stand and the surrounding houses, railway and factories.

1923 was not a happy time for United, with the club stuck in the lower reaches of the Second Division, and Chapman initially struggled to drag the players out of their malaise.

United finished in fourteenth place in the Second Division for the first two seasons that Chapman was in charge and made little headway in the FA Cup.

However, things changed in 1925 and Chapman led United to promotion back into the First Division, when the club finished second to Leicester City. United consolidated their position in the league by finishing ninth in 1926.

Chapman's time at the club ended midway through the following season, when the English FA suspended him from football for improper conduct as manager of Manchester Utd. The FA has never revealed the reason behind this decision, and Chapman was temporarily replaced by player Lal Hilditch, as United finished the campaign in fifteenth place.

For the short time he was in charge, half-back Hilditch became the only player/manager in United's history. He was replaced for the 1927–28 season by former Oldham and Middlesbrough boss Herbert Bamlett, who had also been a football referee earlier in his career.

United suffered a major setback in 1927, when the club's saviour John Henry Davies died suddenly. This brought in a huge period of uncertainty for the club, which was only lifted in 1932, when wealthy Cheshire businessman James Gibson was convinced to pump funds into United and become the club's new chairman.

Scott Duncan managed United for five years, 1932–1937.

Meanwhile, United's fortunes under Bamlett hadn't improved all that much, as they finished in mid-table obscurity for three seasons in a row.

It got worse for United during the 1930–31 season, when they finished bottom of the table, winning just seven of their forty-two league games. Bamlett was duly relieved of his duties in April 1931, with United languishing at the foot of the table.

Club secretary Walter Crickmer was drafted in as manager, as the team began the 1931–32 season back in the Second Division.

Crickmer's United were unable to gain promotion straight away, and they could finish only twelfth. His short stint as manager ended

The 1938–39 team. The Irishmen on the team are Tommy Breen (back row, third from right) and Harry Baird (back row, far right).

that season and United sought the services of Scotsman Scott Duncan.

Duncan became the first non-Englishman to manage United when he took up the reins in 1932 and he brought in a number of Irishmen during his five years in charge.

Half-back Walter McMillen was snapped up from Cliftonville in 1933 and was followed to Old Trafford by the legendary Johnny Carey in 1936. County Louth goalkeeper Thomas Breen, regarded as one of the best goalies in Ireland at the time, also made the move to Manchester from Belfast Celtic in 1936, whilst

forward Harry Baird was brought in from Linfield in 1937.

Old Trafford also went through a transformation around this time, as chairman James Gibson, who had made his fortune manufacturing army uniforms, decided to progress the club both on and off the pitch.

In 1934, a roof was added to the United Road stand for the first time, while roofs were added to the south corners in 1938.

The highlight of the Duncan era came in 1936 when he led United to promotion as champions of the Second Division.

Unfortunately, though, the club's stay in the top flight was all too brief, and they were relegated the following year.

Duncan eventually resigned from Man Utd in October 1937, become manager at Ipswich Town and Walter Crickmer stepped back in, enjoying stunning success by guiding United to promotion at the first time of asking in 1938. He remained manager for the 1938–39 season, as the Old Trafford outfit finished in fourteenth place, but his time at the helm was interrupted by the outbreak of the Second World War.

Although United had become something of a yo-yo team during the years leading up to the Second World War, the club had undergone a number of hugely significant events.

The move to Old Trafford shortly after capturing their first league and FA Cup crowns had ensured they had a home ground as good as any club in the country. Their two league title wins during the early part of the twentieth century also catapulted United into the top tier of successful clubs in the country, capable of attracting some of the best players from around the British Isles.

The uncertainty and chaos brought on by the First World War had interrupted United's march to dominance.

It took the club a long time to develop successfully in the period following the end of that war and many of United's best achievements in the 1920s and 1930s came in the Second Division. Nevertheless, a platform had been set for the club to go on and become one of the most decorated in English football history – with a whole host of Irishmen central to that success.

Seasons when Irishmen were Top Goalscorers

1937–38
Harry Baird – 15 goals
(joint-top scorer with Tommy Bamford)

1967–68
George Best – 32 goals

1969–70
George Best – 23 goals

1970–71
George Best – 21 goals

1971–72
George Best – 26 goals

1973–74
Sammy McIlroy – 6 goals (joint-top scorer with Lou Macari)

1981–82
Frank Stapleton – 13 goals

1982–83
Frank Stapleton – 19 goals

1983–84
Frank Stapleton – 19 goals

Player Profiles

	Thomas Morrison
Place of birth:	Belfast
Date of birth:	16 September 1874
Position:	Forward
Years at United:	1902–1904
Games played:	36
Goals:	8

Belfast-born Thomas Morrison arrived in Manchester having already enjoyed an eventful football career at Glentoran, Burnley and Glasgow Celtic.

He joined Manchester United in December 1902 as the club was undergoing a complete transformation. His new club, which had just recently changed its name from Newton Heath, was endeavouring to find a way out of the Second Division, where it had been stuck for the previous eight years.

Morrison's debut for United came in a Christmas Day clash with local rivals Manchester City in 1902 when 40,000 fans showed up for the game at United's Bank Street ground as Morrison helped his new team to a 1–1 draw.

Remarkably, Morrison played two more games for United in the next forty-eight hours, as a punishing Christmas schedule saw the club play three games in as many days. He scored in the second game, as they drew 2–2 with Blackpool, and was in the team

again a day later when they beat Barnsley 2–1.

This proved to be a decent start to Morrison's United career, although it never reached any great heights after that.

His next goal for the club came in a 3–1 league win over Glassop in January 1903 and, a month later, he scored United's two goals in a 2–2 draw with Doncaster Rovers. Morrison continued his scoring streak throughout the rest of the season, notching up goals in impressive home wins against Leicester Fosse, Burnley and Doncaster Rovers.

United eventually finished the season in fifth place in the Second Division, but had gained some stability after an uncertain period as Newton Heath.

Morrison had helped play his part in United's turnaround in fortunes, but he didn't feature much in his second season at the club.

As United's first real manager Ernest Magnall took charge of the team in 1903, Morrison's appearances on the pitch became less frequent. He played in just nine league games for United during the 1903–04 season and failed to score in any of them.

Perhaps Morrison's greatest highlight at United came in February 1904, when he scored in the club's 2–1 FA Cup win against the highly fancied First Division outfit Notts County.

United finished the season in third place in the Second Division, but it was to be Morrison's last campaign at the club.

19

Outside club football, Morrison was capped seven times for Ireland and scored just the one goal.

In September 1904, he left United to join Colne FC, a club in northwest England. His last game for Manchester United came in a 1–1 draw away to Preston North End in March 1904.

Morrison scored eight goals during his two-year United career.

Other Clubs: Glentoran, Burnley, Glasgow Celtic, Colne FC
International Record: Ireland
Caps: 7
Goals: 1

Mickey Hamill	
Place of birth:	Belfast
Date of birth:	9 January 1889
Position:	Inside-forward
	Half-back
Years at United:	1911–1914
Games played:	60
Goals:	2

Forward Mickey Hamill joined Manchester United in January 1911 as the club was enjoying its first great era under manager Ernest Magnall, who had led United to their first league and FA Cup titles in the previous three years. It was an excellent move for twenty-two-year-old Hamill.

United had snapped him up from Belfast Celtic, after he had spent a brief period on loan at Glasgow Celtic without playing a game. Hamill was made to wait before making his United debut, as his new team were already on the way to claiming their second league title in three seasons in May 1911.

He eventually came into the side at the start of United's new campaign, making his debut in September 1911 in a 1–1 draw away to West Brom.

Hamill did enough to keep his place in the team for the Charity Shield game at Stamford Bridge against FA Cup winners Swindon Town. Hamill gave a scintillating performance in this amazing game that produced twelve goals, as United ran out 8–4 winners. However, he then spent the rest of the season in and out of the side, as United failed to reproduce the form that had made them the most feared team in the country.

The downward trend continued as Hamill played in eight league games in a row that United failed to win, and the club plummeted to the bottom half of the table.

After more than a year at the club, Hamill scored his first goal for United in a 3–1 victory over Blackburn in April 1912, but it was a rare win for the team with him in the side.

United finished the 1911–12 season way back in thirteenth place in the league, before Magnall left the club to manage neighbours Manchester City.

Under John Bentley's stewardship, Hamill's appearances remained sporadic. By the end of 1912, he had only played in three league games as Bentley preferred to use his other forwards

George Anderson, George Wall and Thomas Nuttel.

At the turn of the year, Hamill managed to notch up a goal against Everton but United unfortunately lost the game 4–1. However, the goal helped to keep Hamill in the side as he played in another eleven league games for United that season as they finished impressively in fourth place in the First Division.

Hamill remained part of the United team for the 1913–14 season but United failed to live up to the heights they had enjoyed under Magnall. The club did have an amazing run of eight wins on the trot with Hamill in the side, but their form dipped dramatically in the second half of the season.

The 1913–14 team. Mickey Hamill is on the back row (second from right). The legendary Billy Meredith is seated on the front row, first left.

They struggled to find any kind of form in the league in 1914, finishing way back in fourteenth place, and Hamill failed to score a single goal in the twenty-five games he played that season.

The outbreak of the First World War disrupted Hamill's career with United and he spent much of the next five years playing as a guest in challenge matches for former clubs Belfast Celtic and Glasgow Celtic.

Hamill also played for Ireland seven times between 1912 and 1921, scoring just one goal, which came on his international debut in a 6–1 defeat to England in October 1912.

When the Football League resumed in 1920, Hamill signed up to play for United's main rivals Manchester City. His last game for United had come in a 0–0 draw with Blackburn Rovers at Old Trafford in April 1914.

In the three years he had been at the club, Hamill played in sixty games and scored two goals.

Mickey Hamill passed away in Lisburn on 19 July 1943, at the age of fifty-four.

Other Clubs: Belfast Celtic, Glasgow Celtic, Manchester City, Fall River Marksmen, Boston Wonder Workers, New York Giants
International Record: Ireland
Caps: 7
Goals: 1

Patrick O'Connell	
Place of birth:	Dublin
Date of birth:	8 March 1887
Position:	Central defender
Years at United:	1914–1919
Games played:	35
Goals:	2

Tough defender Patrick O'Connell became Manchester United's first Irish captain when he signed for the club in a £1,000 deal from Hull City in May 1914.

United had just come under the management of former Middlesbrough manager Jack Robson and were trying to repeat the league title success they had enjoyed in 1908 and 1911.

One of Robson's first decisions was to make O'Connell his captain and the Dublin-born defender made his debut in a home game against local rivals Oldham Athletic in September 1914. O'Connell scored that day but United lost the game 3–1.

Three days later, he was in the United side that drew 0–0 in the Manchester derby at Old Trafford. O'Connell had to wait until October and a 3–0 home win over Sunderland to enjoy his first victory with United.

Despite the optimism which came with new manager Robson, United struggled badly in the league that year, winning just one of their next twelve games with O'Connell in the side.

The FA Cup offered little relief as United were dumped out early by Sheffield Wednesday in a 1–0 defeat.

A rare highlight for O'Connell's captaincy came in a 4–1 home win over Bolton Wanderers, but, despite this, United continued to struggle and relegation became a real possibility. However, such woes soon became the least of United's worries as the outbreak of the First World War threatened the continuation of the Football League.

The uncertainty caused by the outbreak of war made many of United's players fear for their futures and some, O'Connell included, took part in a major betting scandal involving players from rival club Liverpool.

As United prepared to play Liverpool in a league game on 2 April 1915, players from both clubs met beforehand to fix the score of the game.

United subsequently won the game 2–0 but a badly missed penalty from O'Connell aroused suspicion. He had stepped forward to take the penalty with the score at 2–0 and hit it well wide of the goal.

When the scandal broke, O'Connell somehow managed to escape punishment. However, three of his team-mates – Sandy Turnbull, Arthur Whalley and Enoch West – received lifetime bans from the Football Association.

If the whole sordid affair had affected O'Connell, he didn't show it, and, just a week later, he scored his second goal for United in a 2–2 draw with Middlesbrough at Old Trafford.

By the end of the season, United had finished in eighteenth place in the league, avoiding relegation by a single point. At this stage, the Football League was suspended for the duration of the war and O'Connell's competitive United career came to a premature end. He remained at the club during the war years and played in a number of challenge games.

On the international scene, O'Connell enjoyed great success with Ireland as they won the 1914 British Home Championships with a 2–1 win over Wales and a stunning 3–0 victory over England. O'Connell captained the Irish team which finally captured the championships with a 1–1 draw against Scotland in Windsor Park in March 1914.

When club football resumed in 1919, O'Connell signed up for Scottish side Dumbarton. His last game for United had been in a 1–0 win over Aston Villa at Old Trafford in April 1915.

When his playing days were over, O'Connell enjoyed a successful career as a manager in Spain, where he won La Liga with Real Betis and he even managed Catalan giants Barcelona.

Patrick O'Connell died in London in 1959, aged seventy-two.

Other Clubs: Belfast Celtic, Sheffield Wednesday, Hull City, Dumbarton, Ashington
International Record: Ireland
Caps: 6
Goals: 0

Davy Lyner	
Place of birth:	Belfast
Date of birth:	9 January 1893
Position:	Outside-left
	Outside-right
Years at United:	1922–1923
Games played:	3
Goals:	0

When experienced forward Davy Lyner signed for Manchester United in August 1922, he already had numerous honours with Irish League club Glentoran under his belt. He arrived at the club as one of eleven signings made by new manager John Chapman in his bid to have United promoted from the Second Division.

However, the 1922–23 season proved a major let-down for United, as they struggled in the league, with Lyner only playing a small part in the first team.

Despite his previous playing experience, and the fact that he could play as either an outside-right or left, Lyner found it difficult to break into a team which had many established forward players.

Lyner's first appearance for United came in September 1922, when they were beaten 2–0 by Coventry City at Highfield Road. He kept his place in the team a week later, but United lost again, this time 2–1 at home to Coventry.

Lyner's only other appearance for United came in another defeat, when his new side lost 2–1 at home to Port Vale in October 1922. It was his last game for the club as he struggled to nail down a permanent place in the first team – though he became a regular in the United reserve team for the months following the Port Vale game.

During his career, Lyner was capped six times for Ireland, making his debut in a 1–1 draw with England in October 1919.

By December 1922, he made the decision to leave Manchester United and signed up for Scottish side Kilmarnock. Lyner continued to play football for another six years and remained constantly on the move, playing for another seven clubs during that time.

Other Clubs: Glentoran, Kilmarnock, Queen's Island, Dunlea, Clydebank, Mid Rhonda, New Brighton
International Record: Ireland
Caps: 6
Goals: 0

Billy Behan	
Place of birth:	Dublin
Date of birth:	8 August 1911
Position:	Goalkeeper
Years at United:	1933–1934
Games played:	1
Goals:	0

Dublin-born goalkeeper Billy Behan may have only played one game for Manchester United, but he proved there was more than one way to become a club legend.

Signed in August 1933 after a career in the League of Ireland with Dublin clubs Shelbourne and Shamrock Rovers, Behan joined a United team that was struggling near the far reaches of the Second Division. Nevertheless, manager Scott Duncan had an abundance of goalkeepers at the club so Behan found his chances in the United side limited.

John Hall and Charles Hillam were the preferred goalkeepers, with Behan the third choice in goal.

Behan's only game for United came in a 2–1 win over Bury at Old Trafford on 3 March 1934. Despite helping United to this win, Behan was back out of the side a week later as Hillam was, once again, chosen in goal.

When the season ended, Behan, frustrated at his lack of opportunities at Old Trafford, returned to Shelbourne in July 1934.

However, this was far from the end of Behan's connection with Old Trafford. When he retired from playing the game in 1936, Behan became a valuable member of United's scouting team, and helped to unearth a number of gems from Ireland. He was responsible for the likes of Liam Whelan, Tony Dunne and Paul McGrath finding their way to Old Trafford, and he remained a scout for United for over forty years.

Behan passed away on 12 November 1991 at the age of eighty.

Other Clubs: Shelbourne, Shamrock Rovers

David Byrne	
Place of birth:	Dublin
Date of birth:	28 April 1906
Position:	Forward
Years at United:	1933–1934
Games played:	4
Goals:	3

Forward David Byrne was snapped up by Manchester United in 1933 from top Dublin football club Shamrock Rovers. He had been a big star in the Rovers side that had won the League of Ireland and FAI Cup on numerous occasions before he made the move to England.

He had even been the league's joint top scorer in 1927 and arrived at Old Trafford with what looked to be a promising career ahead of him.

As it turned out, Byrne would only be at

the club for a little over half a season, in which time he played just four games, but he did manage to score three times.

Byrne joined Manchester United when the club was going through a downturn in fortunes, struggling to make it out of the Second Division. He made an immediate impact by scoring on his debut against local rivals Bury in October 1933.

Unfortunately for Byrne, United lost that game 2–1 and they struggled to find form for the majority of that season.

Byrne's next appearance came on Christmas Day in 1933, when United were beaten 3–1 by Grimsby at Old Trafford. A day later, United had to make the return trip to Grimsby's Blundell Park, as they struggled near the foot of the table. Despite Byrne scoring two goals that day, things were still very grim for United as they lost the match 7–3.

Byrne played one more game for United that year, as they were beaten 4–0 at Old Trafford by Plymouth Argyle.

It proved to be the forward's last game for the club and, in February 1905, he was let go to Coleraine.

In Byrne's absence, United finished the season third from bottom in the Second Division – the club's lowest finish since the start of the Football League.

Other Clubs: Shamrock Rovers, Coleraine

Walter McMillen	
Place of birth:	Belfast
Date of birth:	24 October 1913
Position:	Half-back
Years at United:	1933–1935
Games played:	29
Goals:	2

Manchester United snapped up Belfast-born half-back Walter McMillen from right under the noses of Arsenal in July 1933.

McMillen had made a name for himself in the successful Cliftonville side of the early 1930s, helping them to win the Gold Cup in 1933 and had attracted the attention of Arsenal, whom he had trials with that year.

But he eventually signed up at Old Trafford, where United were under the management of Scott Duncan in the Second Division.

McMillen made his debut for United in September 1933, when he helped his new side to a 4–3 win over Brentford.

His first appearance at Old Trafford was equally successful, as United romped to a 5–2 win over Burnley.

McMillen became a fixture in the side that year, but despite the promising start, United struggled badly and only just avoided relegation by finishing in eighteenth place.

McMillen played a massive part in maintaining United's Second Division status when he scored in a 2–0 win over Port Vale in April 1934. Without that precious win, United would indeed have been relegated to the Third Division for the first time.

By the end of the season, McMillen had appeared in twenty-three of United's league games, but was missing from the side for large parts of the 1934–35 season as United improved sufficiently enough to finish sixth. McMillen played his first game that season on St Stephen's (Boxing) Day as United lost 1–0 to Notts County.

He appeared only three more times for United during his time there, playing mostly as an outside-left.

In his last match in a red shirt, McMillen scored his second goal during a seven-goal thriller with Burnley at Old Trafford. Unfortunately, United lost the game 4–3.

Though he remained at the club for almost two more years, he only played for United's reserve team.

McMillen's time at Old Trafford finally ended in December 1936 when he was transferred to Chesterfield for £2,000.

Other Clubs: Cliftonville, Arsenal, Chesterfield, Millwall, Glentoran, Linfield, Tonbridge
International Record: Ireland
Caps: 7
Goals: 0

Harry Baird	
Place of birth:	Belfast
Date of birth:	17 August 1913
Position:	Striker/Midfielder
Years at United:	1936–1938
Games played:	53
Goals:	18

Forward Harry Baird moved to Manchester United in January 1937 after a successful career with Linfield. He was considered one of the best forwards in Ireland at the time and United manager Scott Duncan had to shell out £3,500 to acquire his services.

Baird went straight into the United first team when he made his debut against Sheffield Wednesday in the same month he had signed for the club, but he could do little to prevent their slide towards relegation from the First Division.

United didn't win in any of the first six games Baird played for them, but he did manage to score his first goal for the club in

a 3–1 defeat to Brentford at Old Trafford.

Baird enjoyed his first moment of glory at United when he scored the winning goal in a 2–1 win over Stoke City in March 1937. He repeated the trick a few weeks later in a 2–1 win over Everton at Old Trafford but the two wins could not stop United being relegated to the Second Division that season.

Under new manager Walter Crickmer, Baird's second season at United was a resounding success.

United ruled the Second Division that year, along with Aston Villa, with Baird in the thick of the action and knocking in plenty of goals.

He scored in a magnificent 7–1 win over Chesterfield in November 1937 and added to this with two more goals in a 4–3 win over Nottingham Forest at Old Trafford in December.

Baird kept his scoring boots on in the FA Cup as he scored in a 3–0 win over Yeovil, whilst he and fellow Irishman Jackie Carey got United's goals in a 2–2 draw with Barnsley. United won the replay 1–0 thanks to another goal from Baird. Unfortunately, United could not keep their Cup run going, and they were knocked out in a 2–0 defeat to Brentford with Baird in the side.

That Cup defeat did little to stop United's march on to promotion, however, and Baird helped them to a 4–0 win over West Ham in March with another two goals.

Baird then scored in each of his next three games, as United closed in on regaining a spot in the First Division.

By the end of the season, Baird had finished as United's joint top goal scorer with Tommy Bramford on fifteen goals each, as the team finished second in the league to Aston Villa.

Despite this success, Baird was soon on his way out of Old Trafford when he was transferred to Huddersfield in September 1938.

His last game for United was in a 2–0 win over Bury, while his last goal at Old Trafford had been in a 3–1 win over Bradford PA in April 1938.

Harry Baird died on 22 May 1973, at the age of sixty.

Other Clubs: Bangor, Linfield, Huddersfield Town, Ipswich Town
International Record: Ireland
Caps: 1
Goals: 0

Tommy Breen	
Place of birth:	Drogheda
Date of birth:	27 April 1912
Position:	Goalkeeper
Years at United:	1936–1939
Games played:	71
Goals:	0

Described as one of the most talented goal-keepers to ever come out of Ireland, County Louth man Thomas Breen signed for Manchester United in November 1936.

Breen had started his football career playing as a forward but, after serious injury forced him to give up playing outfield, he decided to become a goalkeeper. He proved a revelation in his new position and soon found himself playing in goal for top side Belfast Celtic, from where he was transferred to Manchester United.

Breen was drafted in for his United debut in November 1936, after regular goalkeeper Roy John had conceded eleven goals in his previous two games.

Unfortunately, Breen's first action for United was one he would rather forget as he was beaten in his very first minute in goal in a 2–1 defeat to Leeds Utd.

Breen put this early disappointment behind him to become United's first-choice keeper throughout the rest of the 1936–37 season. It was not a happy time for United, however, as they struggled badly in the First Division and were relegated.

That season, United won just seven of the twenty-six league games when Breen was in goal and he managed to keep just two clean sheets during that time.

However, Breen's United side proved a much different proposition in the Second Division as they set about regaining a place in the top flight.

With fellow Irishmen Jackie Carey and Harry Baird in the side, Breen helped United to finish second to Aston Villa at the end of the 1937–38 season to gain promotion to the First Division.

Breen played in thirty-three of United's league games that season, keeping seven clean sheets, as great club servant Walter Crickmer enjoyed success in his second stint as manager.

When United returned to action in the First Division, Breen's place in the side was under threat from fellow goalkeepers John Breedon and Norman Tapkin and Breen played just six games that season, keeping one clean sheet, as they finished in fourteenth place.

Breen was also selected to represent Ireland on the international front.

At the time, the two football associations in Ireland – the Belfast based IFA and the Dublin based FAI – both claimed jurisdiction over Ireland. As a result, Breen played for both associations and amassed a total of eighteen caps.

Meanwhile, the outbreak of the Second World War disrupted Breen's time at Manchester United and he returned to Ireland to play for Belfast Celtic and their arch rivals Linfield.

When the war ended and the Football

Tommy Breen in training during the 1936–37 season.

League resumed in 1946, United's new manager Matt Busby had hoped that Breen would return to Manchester to play for them, but Breen decided to remain in Ireland and signed to play for Shamrock Rovers.

It's debatable if this was the right move by Breen as United went on to enjoy FA Cup glory the following year under Busby.

Breen's last game for United had been in a 1–1 draw with Huddersfield Town on 1 April 1939. In the seventy-one games he kept goal for Manchester United, Breen managed to keep sixteen clean sheets.

Other Clubs: Newry Town, Belfast Celtic, Linfield, Shamrock Rovers, Glentoran
International Record: Ireland IFA & FAI
Caps: 18 (13–IFA) (5–FAI)
Goals: 0

Johnny Carey	
Place of birth:	Dublin
Date of birth:	23 February 1919
Position:	Defender/Midfielder
	Forward
Years at United:	1936–1953
Games played:	344
Goals:	17
Hounours:	First Division (1952);
	FA Cup (1948)

Johnny (Jackie) Carey joined Manchester United in 1936 at a time when the club was languishing in the Second Division. However, the versatile Dubliner would go on to have a glorious career with United which, despite the interruption of the Second World War, earned him a number of major honours.

Carey was first spotted when he was playing for local side St James's Gate by United's Dublin scout Billy Behan and, at seventeen, he was brought to Old Trafford by United chief scout Louis Rocca for a modest fee of £250.

He was initially signed as an inside-left, but was in competition with another famous United player of the time, Stan Pearson, for this position.

Carey made his United debut in a 2–1 defeat to Southampton in Division Two in August 1937 and became a regular in the United side that eventually gained promotion to the First Division at the end of the season. He remained a regular in the United team,

playing their first season back in the First Division. However, it was far from a spectacular season for United, and they finished fourteenth, but Carey's promising career was halted by the outbreak of war.

When the war ended, Carey returned to Manchester United, where new manager Matt Busby instantly made him captain of the team.

It was the first of many inspired decisions that Busby would make during his managerial career, as Carey went on to become one of United's greatest captains.

Although he now preferred to play as a defender, Carey could play in practically every position on the pitch and even famously played in goal for United on one occasion.

In their first season back playing football, United finished second in the league, with Carey playing in thirty of their forty-two games as they lost out on the title by a point to Liverpool.

One of Carey's proudest moments as United captain came a year later, in 1948 when he led the team out at Wembley to take on Blackpool in the FA Cup final. In a brilliant game of football, Carey's United side twice had to come from behind before winning 4–2, as he claimed the first major honour of his professional football career.

Carey's excellent performances in the United shirt had not gone unnoticed as he was named the Professional Football Writers Player of the Year in 1949 as the Red Devils finished second in the league for the third year running.

Carey was another of a group of Irish players who played for the two Ireland teams

Johnny Carey.

which were run by the rival associations the FAI and the IFA. He played most of his football for the FAI team, which he captained nineteen times, scoring three goals.

Back in club football, Carey eventually helped United end their run of second place finishes by actually winning the league in 1952. In doing so, Carey became the first non-Englishman to captain an English team to both the league and FA Cup titles.

He made another appearance at Wembley for the Charity Shield in September 1952, when United beat Newcastle Utd 4–2, and remained on as the United club captain until he retired from football in May 1953.

Carey was held in such high regard at United, that he was immediately offered a position as a coach at the club on his retirement as a player, but he turned it down in favour of becoming manager at Blackburn Rovers.

Carey's illustrious career at Old Trafford has put him down as one of United's greatest ever servants.

Johnny Carey died on 22 February 1995, at the age of seventy-five.

Other Clubs: St James's Gate
International Record: Ireland FAI & IFA
Caps: 36 (29–FAI) (6–IFA)
Goals: 3

Matt Busby leads out his Busby Babes for the 1957 FA Cup final.

The First Busby Era

(1946-1958)

When the Football League resumed in 1946 following the ravages of the Second World War, Manchester United returned to First Division action without even a ground to play in.

Old Trafford had become the victim of relentless German bombing in March 1941, rendering it incapable of hosting a football match until 1949. During this time, United played their home games at cross-town rivals Manchester City's Maine Road ground, although this didn't seem to affect United all that much.

United began the 1946–47 season under the charge of new manager Matt Busby, who was brought to United by chairman James Gibson after the tenacious Scotsman's successful playing career with Manchester City and Liverpool.

Busby had initially been earmarked for a coaching role at Liverpool but, after a fallout with the hierarchy at Anfield, he was let go from the club and Liverpool's loss proved to be Manchester United's gain as Busby went on to oversee one of the most glorious periods in the club's history.

As early as his first season in charge, Busby showed his incredible management skills by guiding United to a second place finish in the league behind his old club Liverpool.

Dublin-born defender Jackie Carey, who signed for United before the war, had returned to the club and was a mainstay in Busby's team. In fact, one of Busby's first decisions as Manchester United manager was to make Carey the club captain, an honour the Dubliner kept until his retirement from the game in 1953.

Busby proved the impressive start to his management career was no fluke when he guided United to runners-up spot in the league again in 1948. Better was to come for United that season, though, when they landed their first piece of major silverware in three decades by winning the FA Cup. With Carey as captain, United embarked on an incredible

Matt Busby talking tactics with some of his players, 1946. Jackie Carey is second from left.

Cup run that year which included a third-round 6–4 victory over Aston Villa and culminated in a 4–2 final victory over Blackpool.

Busby's United had laid down their mark and would go on to become one of the best teams in the country over the next decade.

United finished second in the league for a third time in 1949, when they made their return to a redeveloped Old Trafford.

At the end of the Second World War, the British War Commission had granted Manchester United £4,800 to remove the debris from the bombed-out ground and £17,474 to rebuild the stands. The stadium was reopened for the beginning of the 1949–50 season, but the stands didn't have any cover.

The return to their old stomping ground proved a massive boost to United, as they

Captain Jackie Carey with the FA Cup – the club won the competition for a second time in 1948.

were now able to play home games in front of crowds of nearly 50,000.

United's first game back at Old Trafford was played on 24 August 1949, and 41,748 spectators witnessed a 3–0 victory over Bolton Wanderers.

The club's decent form in the league continued when they, once again, finished second in 1951, before finally capturing the elusive league title twelve months later.

Sadly, the club chairman James Gibson was not around to enjoy the title-winning season, as he had died from a heart attack in 1951.

Gibson was replaced as chairman by former England international footballer Harold Hardman, who would remain in the position for the next fifteen years. However, James Gibson's wife Lillian continued to be the largest shareholder at Manchester United until her death in 1971.

Captain Jackie Carey was the only Irishman to enjoy the great United title success of 1952. Others would soon follow him to the club, however, as Busby began the process of bringing in the best young footballers from around the British Isles.

Talented young half-back Jackie Blanchflower was brought to Old Trafford in 1949 and was followed to the club by Noel McFarlane, Paddy Kennedy, John Scott and Liam Whelan within the next four years.

The man entrusted with the duty of developing the young players at Man Utd was coach Jimmy Murphy, a Welshman with Irish ancestry. His enthusiasm and incredible ability to get the best from young players was a huge part of the success of Manchester United over the twenty years of Busby's tenure.

United lost their grip on the First Division title in 1954 when they could only finish in eighth position. Nevertheless, Busby's continued development of the youth side of the club meant it was only a matter of time before a new great first team would come to fruition.

The club also continued the reconstruction of its Old Trafford ground as a roof was restored to the Main Stand in 1954 and, soon after, the three remaining stands were covered. The club also invested in the installation of proper floodlighting.

By 1955, top-class players – such as Duncan Edwards, Dennis Viollet and Jackie Blanchflower – had come through the ranks of the youth team to take their place in an exciting new-look United senior team. A year later, they were joined by the imperious Liam Whelan and Bobby Charlton as Busby led United to their second league crown under his reign.

The fast-flowing and free-style attacking football that Busby had brought to this extremely young United side – which had gained the nickname 'The Busby Babes' – made them one of the best teams to have ever played in England. They won the league in 1956, scoring over eighty goals and improved on that a year later by scoring 103 goals as they won the league by twelve points.

Busby had developed the basis of a side that looked destined to dominate English football for the next decade.

The emergence of both Jackie Blanchflower

and Liam Whelan in this magnificent United side ensured the Old Trafford club had a huge and ever-growing fan base in Ireland.

United's scintillating style of play had not gone unnoticed on the continent either, where they had become one of the most feared teams in Europe. The club had made it to the semi-finals of the European Cup in 1957, before bowing out to the all-conquering Spanish giants Real Madrid. However, by the start of the 1957–58 season, Busby's young side were being tipped by many to overtake Madrid as the top team in Europe.

United's fans were certainly enjoying their taste of European football, and home games at Old Trafford were attracting crowds of up to 60,000.

Irish fans were given a glimpse of this brilliant United team when they travelled to Dublin in September 1957 to take on Shamrock Rovers in the European Cup. In one of the best displays of football ever seen on Irish soil, United romped to a 6–0 win.

The club's popularity in Ireland was at an all-time high as they entered the new year of 1958 determined to retain their league title

Roger Byrne, the United captain, holds the First Division trophy above his head after the presentation at Old Trafford, 1956.

and also capture a first European crown. But the great dream of the 'Busby Babes' came to a tragic and shuddering halt on an icy German airport runway in 1958.

Returning from a triumphant European Cup tie in Belgrade on 6 February 1958, the chartered aeroplane carrying the United team back to Manchester crashed on the runway of Munich's Riem airport.

The crash claimed the lives of eight United players, including Dublin's favourite son Liam Whelan.

While Busby struggled for his own life after the crash, he eventually came around to the horrific reality that his great United team had lost the talents of Duncan Edwards, Liam Whelan, Geoff Bent, David Pegg, Eddie Colman, Roger Byrne, Mark Jones and Tommy Taylor.

> "If the worst happens,
> I am ready for death.
> I hope we all are."

The tragic last words of Liam Whelan, a Munich Air Disaster victim.

The Busby Babes, 1957. (back row, l–r) Duncan Edwards, Billy Foulkes, Mark Jones, Ray Wood, Eddie Colman, David Pegg (front row, l–r) John Berry, Liam Whelan, Roger Byrne, Tommy Taylor, Dennis Viollet.

Twenty-three people in total lost their lives in the tragedy, including United's club secretary Walter Crickmer, chief coach Bert Walley and trainer Tom Curry.

Incredibly, United were back in action within a fortnight of the disaster, and temporary first-team manager Jimmy Murphy even led them to the FA Cup final in 1958, where they lost 2–0 to a Nat Lofthouse-inspired Bolton Wanderers.

The Munich Air Disaster was a tragedy that would have broken many other managers and many other clubs. Not so Matt Busby or Manchester United. Both would recover from the scars of Munich to rise once again and become kings of Europe within a decade.

When Manchester Utd Played in Ireland

Shamrock Rovers 0–6 Manchester Utd

European Cup

Dalymount Park, 25 September 1957

When League of Ireland champions Shamrock Rovers were drawn to play the mighty Manchester United in the preliminary round of the European Cup in 1957, excitement around the country reached fever pitch.

Matt Busby's star-studded side had blazed a trail across England, winning two successive First Division titles and playing some of the best football ever seen in the country.

Rovers themselves were no slouches, and had won numerous league titles and cup competitions throughout the 1950s and were by far the best team in Ireland at the time.

Despite United being red-hot favourites to win, manager Matt Busby took no chances and even travelled to Dublin a fortnight before the game to spy on his opponents. He was spotted on an extremely wet Wednesday evening on 11 September, in the crowd at Dalymount Park, keeping a watchful eye on Rovers as they beat Dublin rivals Drumcondra 1–0 after extra time to win the President's Cup.

When Busby returned to Dublin with his squad two weeks later, the rain was still falling. In fact, it was so bad that it was decided to start the game at Dalymount at the earlier time of 5.45 p.m., and many believed the weather would give Rovers their best chance of success.

The inclement weather failed to deter the thousands of fans who packed into Dalymount that night, eagerly awaiting their opportunity to see one of the first superstar sides to come to Ireland.

The official attendance that night was recorded at 46,000, but with lots of fans skipping into the game over walls and under turnstiles, the actual figure was many thousands more.

For their part, Rovers named a strong side, which included former 'Busby Babe' Tommy Hamilton up front, flanked by player/manager Paddy Coad and Paddy Ambrose.

But it was the stars on the United team who everybody had come to see, and Busby didn't disappoint. He picked the strongest team he had available to him, including Irishmen Jackie Blanchflower and Liam Whelan, alongside the brilliant Duncan Edwards and forward Dennis Viollet.

When the game kicked off, Rovers were playing against a strong wind, but more than held their own in the first forty-five minutes against their illustrious opponents. Though they did have to rely on the excellence of their goalkeeper Eamon D'Arcy as he made two great saves from Whelan and one from David Pegg.

Shay Keogh and Gerry Mackey in the Rovers' defence were difficult to pass, whilst Ronnie Nolan played an excellent game at wing-half, getting in tackles and using the ball cleverly.

Unfortunately for Rovers, they were unable to make much headway up front, as Duncan Edwards played a spellbinding game in front of United's central defenders Banchflower and Byrne. Fred Goodwin also stuck to Paddy Coad like a limpet, limiting his usefulness to the Rovers side.

Rovers' rearguard was breached just once during the first half when United made the breakthrough through Tommy Taylor, who latched on to a pass from David Pegg in the thirty-sixth minute and chipped the ball over the head of D'Arcy in the Rovers' goal.

The home side went in 1–0 down at half-time but still had high hopes that they could make something of the tie. But those hopes were shattered in a blistering six-minute spell at the start of the second half, when a Dublin man broke the hearts of Shamrock Rovers with a quick fire double.

Liam Whelan took centre stage in the second half, when he doubled United's lead with a goal in the fifty-first minute. The Cabra-born inside-forward broke into a gap made by John Berry's intelligent pass and trapped the ball with his knee before guiding it home past D'Arcy.

Rovers barely had time to catch their breath before Whelan was in again to make it 3–0. This time, he rose gracefully in the box on fifty-seven minutes to head home a cross from Pegg.

Rovers didn't let their heads drop, however, and should have scored two goals of their own.

Player/manager Paddy Coad missed a glorious chance after being set up by fellow forward Paddy Ambrose and, just minutes later, they came even closer. After Wood in the United goal punched out a centre from Liam Tuohy, Noel Peyton slammed the ball back towards the United goal but it rebounded off the crossbar, despite every Shamrock Rovers' fan willing it to go in.

United responded to this let-off by scoring another three goals late in the game, as the part-time Rovers' players began to tire. First, Tommy Taylor got his second of the game after D'Arcy failed to cut out a cross from Dennis Viollet in the eightieth minute.

United were now passing the ball with ease as Rovers struggled and more goals looked inevitable in the remaining few minutes. Berry got United's fifth goal in the eighty-fifth minute and David Pegg scored another a minute later to complete the rout.

A 6–0 scoreline was tough on Shamrock Rovers, particularly as they should have had a couple of goals of their own.

Afterwards, Paddy Coad said his players would learn a lesson from the game and he was proved right for the return leg two weeks later, when his Rovers team put in an heroic performance at Old Trafford, losing only 3–2.

United marched on from the tie with a 9–2 aggregate win and were considered one of the big favourites to win the European Cup that season. However, the Munich Air Disaster in February 1958 robbed Busby's side of that chance and a depleted United team were eventually beaten by AC Milan in the semi-finals.

The fact that five of the eight United players who died in the tragedy had played in the Dalymount Park tie against Shamrock Rovers, made this European Cup clash even more poignant for those who were there to witness it.

REFEREE: M.L. van Nuffel (Belgium)
ATTENDANCE: 46,000

D'Arcy

Burke   Mackey

Nolan   Keogh   Hennessey

Coad   Peyton

Ambrose   Tuohy

Hamilton

Taylor   Viollet

Berry   Whelan   Pegg

Goodwin   Blanchflower   Edwards

Foulkes   Byrne

Wood

Manchester United

Player Profiles

Ignatius Feehan	
Place of birth:	Dublin
Date of birth:	17 August 1926
Position:	Goalkeeper
Years at United:	1948–1950
Games played:	14
Goals:	0

Ignatius 'Sonny' Feehan was part of the first wave of Irish players to join Manchester United under the legendary Matt Busby when he was brought to the club from Waterford in November 1948.

In so doing, he also became the first post-war Irishman to play in goal for Manchester United when he made his debut against Huddersfield Town a year later.

Feehan's debut couldn't have gone better as a strong United side strolled to a 6–0 win over Huddersfield at Old Trafford. However, Feehan's chances remained limited, as Busby had an array of keepers to choose from.

Feehan was vying for the number one jersey with both Joseph Lancaster and John Crompton and only really got one chance to have an extended run in the team. He played in five games in succession during December 1949, and United won three of them and lost just once.

Feehan kept his place in goal as United started their FA Cup campaign in early 1950 with a game against Weymouth. He had an easy afternoon and United scored four times to clock up an expected win.

Feehan also played in goal as United beat Portsmouth 3–1 in the FA Cup a month later, but lost his place to Crompton as United crashed out of the cup in a 2–0 defeat to Chelsea. He played three more league games for United that season as Busby led the club to fourth place in the First Division.

However, Feehan's days at United were numbered when Busby shelled out just over £11,000 for QPR's shot-stopper Reg Allen in June 1950 and, before the new season came around, Feehan had been sold to Northampton Town for £565. His last game for United was in a 2–0 loss to Birmingham City in April 1950.

During his only season at Old Trafford, Feehan played in fourteen games and kept four clean sheets.

Other Clubs: Waterford Utd, Northampton

Jackie Blanchflower	
Place of birth:	Belfast
Date of birth:	7 March 1933
Position:	Midfielder
Years at United:	1951–1958
Games played:	117
Goals:	27
Honours:	First Division
	(1956, 1957)

Jackie Blanchflower was another magnificent young Manchester Utd player whose career was cruelly defined by the Munich Air Disaster in 1958. An original member of the 'Busby Babes', Belfast-born Blanchflower looked set to win major European honours with the club until the plane crash ended his career through injury.

Signed by Matt Busby as a sixteen-year-old in 1949, Blanchflower was part of the very successful United youth team that won a succession of FA Youth Cups. His older brother Danny, also a professional footballer, served as captain of Tottenham Hotspur.

The talented defender had arrived at the club around the same time as Busby was acquiring the services of Duncan Edwards, Dennis Viollet and Billy Foulkes. Bobby Charlton and Liam Whelan arrived soon after, forming the basis of a future senior team that would beat all before them in England.

Blanchflower made his debut for the United senior team in a 0–0 draw with Liverpool in 1951, but it was almost two years before he would play again. He finally established himself in the United team in the 1953–54 season as Busby's new-look United side finished fourth in the league.

Blanchflower was a very versatile player who had started his football career playing as an inside-forward. However, Matt Busby chose to play him at centre-half, recognising his excellent aerial power and great positioning.

He was also capable of scoring his fair share of goals, and scored three in two games for United at the beginning of the 1954–55 season as the Red Devils won six of their first eight games in their bid to win the league for the second time. As it was, United could only

Jackie Blanchflower making a save as the stand-in goalkeeper for United during the 1957 FA Cup final against Aston Villa.

finish fifth that season and Chelsea won the league, but they would make no mistake a year later.

Blanchflower was a key member of Busby's team that took the First Division by storm, winning the league with eleven points to spare over nearest rivals Blackpool.

With confidence coursing through their veins, Busby's Babes played even better football the following season, scoring 103 goals in the league and winning the title with a twelve-point margin.

United also marched on to the FA Cup final in 1957, when Blanchflower's amazing versatility proved very useful. The young Belfast man was forced to spend most of the Cup final against Aston Villa in goal, after United keeper Ray Wood was injured early on. Unfortunately, United could not complete the double under Busby, as Villa ran out 2–1 winners.

Blanchflower was back to his regular out-field position at the beginning of the 1957–58 season, when United were expected to pick up even more honours. Busby's big goal at this stage was to win the European Cup.

Blanchflower was in the United team that beat Shamrock Rovers 6–0 in Dublin in September 1957 as they began what they hoped would be a successful European Cup campaign. He also played the night United beat Dukla Prague 3–0 at Old Trafford as they advanced to a meeting with Red Star Belgrade in early 1958.

Blanchflower was not in the United team for the home leg at Old Trafford in January but was part of the squad which flew to Belgrade a month later. After United secured the draw which saw them through to the semi-finals, Blanchflower was on the plane which crashed into the runway in Munich. He was one of the lucky survivors, but the injuries he sustained that night finished his career as a professional footballer. He suffered a fractured pelvis, arms and legs – his right arm was nearly severed – and crushed kidneys.

He tried to return to football, but never made a full recovery. Doctors had advised him not to return to the game because of fears that he would damage his kidney and, a year later, Blanchflower retired from football. His last league appearance for Manchester United had been in a 4–3 defeat to Tottenham in November 1957.

His enforced retirement also meant that he also missed out on Northern Ireland's appearance at the 1958 World Cup finals, though he had been part of the team that recorded a historic 2–1 win over Italy at Windsor Park that had clinched their place at the finals in Sweden.

Jackie Blanchflower died on 2 September 1998, at the age of sixty-five.

Other Clubs: Boyland FC
International Record: Northern Ireland
Caps: 12
Goals: 1

John Scott	
Place of birth:	Belfast
Date of birth:	22 December 1933
Position:	Forward
Years at United:	1950–1956
Games played:	3
Goals:	0

Flying winger John 'Jackie' Scott joined Manchester United as a seventeen-year-old apprentice in December 1950. Signed from Ormond Star in Belfast, Scott formed part of Busby's exciting revolution at Old Trafford.

Visionary Busby had began the process of putting together one of the best youth set-ups seen at any football club in the world and Scott was one of those youngsters who first caught his eye.

Unfortunately for Scott, Busby had also unearthed a plethora of other top-class teens who would surpass him at Old Trafford and go on to form the legendary 'Busby Babes'.

With an array of attacking talent coming through the youth ranks at Old Trafford, Scott found his opportunities at United

extremely limited. Busby gave him his first-team debut in October 1952, but Scott's United side were beaten 6–2 that day by Wolves. Scott made his home debut a week later against Stoke City, but was again on the losing side, as United slumped to a 2–0 defeat.

They were the only two games that Scott played for United that season as the club finished eighth in the First Division and he didn't appear again in the United first team for almost four years.

He was in the unlucky position of being too old to play for United's phenomenal youth team at the time which captured five FA Youth Cups in a row, but Busby called him back into the side in January 1956, when the champions-elect suffered a rare loss, going down 2–1 to Preston.

That was the last time Scott featured for United who went on that year to claim their first of two league titles in a row. Scott departed Old Trafford in June 1956 when he signed for Grimsby Town.

He was part of the Northern Ireland squad which made it to the quarter-finals of the 1958 World Cup with a superb performance in Sweden.

After his playing career was over, Scott settled in Manchester, where he died in June 1978, aged just forty-five.

Other Clubs: Boyland, Ormond Star, Grimsby Town, York City, Margate
International Record: Northern Ireland
Caps: 2
Goals: 0

Noel McFarlane	
Place of birth:	Wicklow
Date of birth:	20 December 1934
Position:	Forward
Years at United:	1952–1956
Games played:	1
Goals:	0

County Wicklow teenager Noel McFarlane joined the massed ranks of Irish youngsters signing for Manchester United in the early 1950s when he made his way to Old Trafford in April 1952. He was yet another youngster United coach Jimmy Murphy had in mind for his prodigious youth teams, which were beating all before them at the time.

Yet, as a forward, McFarlane was another to suffer because of the enormous wealth of talent that manager Matt Busby was bringing through the club. He did enjoy FA Youth Cup success in 1953 as part of the outstanding team that won the final with a comprehensive 9–3 aggregate score over Wolves.

After this, McFarlane spent the majority of his time playing in the reserves, patiently waiting for his chance in the first team.

When it arrived in 1954, it was for the briefest of moments. McFarlane made his United debut on 13 February 1954, playing in the same side as Jackie Blanchflower, Duncan Edwards and Dennis Viollet, when the club played Tottenham and beat them 2–0 before finishing fourth in the league.

It was the only time he would taste first-team action, as players began to come through from the youth ranks.

McFarlane stayed with the club for two more years, before moving back to Ireland in June 1956 to play for Waterford Utd.

Other Clubs: Waterford Utd

Patrick Kennedy	
Place of birth:	Dublin
Date of birth:	19 October 1934
Position:	Full-back
Years at United:	1952–1956
Games played:	1
Goals:	0

Full-back Patrick Kennedy made the move to Old Trafford from his junior club Johnville in February 1952. It was a great time to be signing for United as, just a few months later, they were crowned league champions for the first time under Matt Busby.

Behind the scenes, in the youth and reserve team set-up, all the work was being done to create a team would go on to dominate through the later stages of the 1950s.

Kennedy's first duty when he arrived at United was to play in the youth team, as he waited to be called up to the senior ranks. He was part of the same youth side as Duncan Edwards, David Pegg and Liam Whelan that won the inaugural FA Youth Cup in 1953.

Kennedy received his call from manager Matt Busby to play in the senior team in October 1954 when he was drafted into the team for a game against Wolves at Molineux, which United lost 4–2. It was the only action Kennedy was to see that season as United finished the campaign in fifth place.

The following season, United roared to their second league title under Busby but

Patrick Kennedy.

Kennedy was not part of the team. He was finding it difficult to break into United's star-studded side and was eventually transferred to Blackburn Rovers in August 1956.

When his playing career was over, Kennedy settled in Urmston, close to Old Trafford.

He died at the Trafford General Hospital on 18 March 2007, aged seventy-three.

Other Clubs: Blackburn Rovers, Southampton, Oldham

Liam Whelan	
Place of birth:	Dublin
Date of birth:	1 April 1935
Position:	Winger/Forward
Years at United:	1953–1958
Games played:	96
Goals:	52
Honours:	First Division
	(1956, 1957)

It is hard not to think of how much more Liam Whelan could have accomplished on the football field had his life not been cut so tragically short by the Munich Air Disaster.

Signed by Manchester United as an eighteen-year-old from Dublin club Home Farm in 1953, Whelan spent five years at Old Trafford and achieved what many other players could never have achieved in a lifetime.

Tall and somewhat ungainly, Whelan proved to be a deceptively skilful player with a phenomenal eye for goal. He joined Manchester United as Matt Busby was putting together one of the most talented teams to ever come out of England.

It is to Whelan's immense credit that he became a central figure within this magnificent squad of players which had captured two league titles in the two years before the Munich tragedy.

Playing as an inside-forward, Whelan's first duty at United was to help the youth team win the FA Youth Cup with a comprehensive 7–1 first-leg win over Wolves. He continued his development with the youth team throughout the following season, before Busby eventually gave him his first-team debut in 2–0 league win away to Preston in March 1955.

Whelan never looked back after this as he scored on his league debut against Sheffield Utd in a home game United won 5–0.

He kept his place in the team for the next five matches as United finished the season fifth in the league.

Whelan was in and out of the side during the 1955–56 season, as Busby juggled around the wealth of talent he had at his disposal. The young Dubliner did still play in fourteen league games and scored four goals, as the team romped to the First Division title, a clear eleven points ahead of nearest rivals Blackpool.

This was the start of something truly beautiful for United – and for Whelan.

United retained their title the following season, playing some fantastic football that saw them score over 100 goals in their forty-two league games. For Whelan, it was his best season, and he scored twenty-four goals in thirty-nine league games, as he amassed thirty-three goals in all competitions.

One of those goals was a magnificent solo effort against Spanish side Athletic Bilboa in a European Cup tie which United eventually won 6–5 over the two legs.

Whelan had also helped himself to two goals in a 10–0 home win for United against Belgian club Anderlecht in an earlier round of the same competition.

It eventually took the brilliance of Real Madrid to knock United out of the European Cup at the semi-final stage that year, with Whelan playing in both games, as United lost 5–3 on aggregate.

United began the 1957–58 season as over-whelming favourites to retain their First Division title and were also considered a very strong bet to win the European Cup.

Whelan started the season in brilliant fashion, scoring a hat-trick in a 3–0 win away to Leicester City. Five more goals followed for him, as United won six of their first nine league games, before travelling to Dublin for a historic European Cup game against Shamrock Rovers at Dalymount Park.

Whelan was part of the United team that tore strips off Rovers that night, scoring two goals, as the Red Devils ran out 6–0 winners.

He remained in the side as United coasted past Dukla Prague in their next European Cup encounter and as they kept up their march for a third league crown in a row.

But his place in the team was soon under threat from none other than Bobby Charlton, and Whelan found himself out of the United first eleven by the turn of the year.

In fact, Whelan's last ever game for Manchester United was the 1–0 defeat to Chelsea at Old Trafford on 14 December 1957.

Despite this, he was still an important member of Busby's squad and was on the plane for their European Cup clash with Red Star Belgrade on 5 February. Tragically, he was one of the eight United players to perish when the plane bringing the team home crashed, cutting short the life and career of a young man who had so much more to offer.

Whelan's strike rate of fifty-two goals in ninety-eight games for United is comparable to the scoring records of any of the best strikers who have ever played the game.

Whelan's untimely death meant that he only got to play in four games for Ireland, making his debut in a 4–1 win over Holland on 10 May 1956.

As Ireland's greatest footballing hero at the time, Whelan's funeral at Glasnevin Cemetery was one of the biggest seen in Dublin at the time. As an appreciation of his wonderful achievements at Manchester United, Liam Whelan has a bridge named after him in his native Cabra in North Dublin.

Other Clubs: Home Farm
International Record: Republic of Ireland
Caps: 4
Goals: 0

Liam Whelan.

Scouts

It takes more than just financial clout for a club to continue developing teams capable of winning league titles and major European honours.

As United's two legendary managers Sir Matt Busby and Sir Alex Ferguson have proved, it can be just as important for any successful club to produce its own home-grown talent. But for this to flourish, the club must also have a first-class scouting network in place.

It is United's great fortune that the club has had many excellent scouts, with an intuitive ability to pinpoint youngsters who will ultimately make the grade at Old Trafford.

For the best part of the past century, the club was indebted to two great Irish talent spotters, who sent a conveyor belt of talented young players through the Old Trafford doors. Between them, Belfast scout Bob Bishop and Dublin's Billy Behan helped almost every great Irish player who donned the red shirt.

In Northern Ireland, wily old scout Bob Bishop unearthed the talents of a skinny teen by the name of George Best in 1961. After watching a fifteen-year-old Best torment a team of men two and three years older than him, Bishop had no hesitation in recommending the East Belfast kid to Manchester United. In a now famous telegram sent to Matt Busby, Bishop, a man normally reserved in his praise of young players, declared: 'I think I have found you a genius.'

Even before he had discovered Best, Bishop's work on the ground for United was unrelenting. He had been the brains behind the Boyland FC club, an Under-18 side he set up in Belfast which produced a stream of players for Man Utd. Sammy McIlroy found his way to Old Trafford through Bishop and the brilliant Norman Whiteside followed a decade later.

Meanwhile in the Republic, Dublin-based Billy Behan, a former United goalkeeper from the 1930s, beavered away for forty years producing young talent for his old club.

In 1936, just two years after leaving United, Behan took up the job as chief scout for the club in Ireland. One of his first duties was to send the renowned Jackie Carey to Old Trafford and he was also responsible for Liam Whelan's emergence in the Busby Babes of the 1950s.

Other players to benefit from Behan's sterling work were John Giles and full-back Tony Dunne.

The United team of the 1980s was blessed with the defensive talents of Dublin duo Paul McGrath and Kevin Moran, both of whom were brought to Manchester by Behan.

By the time these two hugely respected scouts retired from their positions in the 1980s, they had created an Irish legacy at Manchester United that continues to benefit both the club and the country to this day.

Academy

In more recent times, Manchester United has endeavoured to spread the appeal of the club in Ireland with the establishment of a well-run coaching academy. Schoolboy clubs from across Northern Ireland and the Republic have benefited, as teens are put through their paces by experienced United coaches.

In Northern Ireland, it has been run under the watchful eye of United's chief scout Eddie Coulter, who has unearthed a number of top international players including Keith Gillespie and David Healy.

Eddie, a devout United fan who became the club's top scout in Northern Ireland in 1985, says it is still a huge honour to work for the club he loves. 'I remember Bob Bishop stating one time that he had the name and phone number of the man who would replace him as United's scout in his wallet,' Eddie said. 'What I didn't know at the time was that man would be me and I have been delighted to have had such a close association with a club I have always supported.'

During his time as scout, Eddie has watched thousands of schoolboy football games all over Northern Ireland and he says the work of the Manchester Utd academy in the country is now starting to bear fruit.

Of the 2008 United squad, Eddie predicts a big future in the game for tall central defender Jonny Evans and combative Derry midfielder Darron Gibson.

'Jonny and Darron were spotted and came through the academy over here before joining up with United. They are two very talented young players who have a great chance of making it at the club. 'Another young Northern Ireland fella with a great future is defender Craig Cathcart. He is currently out on loan from United but if he continues his progression he will have every chance of succeeding at the club.'

In the Republic, Dublin-based scout Joe Corcoran scours the country on the look-out for new United stars, whilst the development of the Manchester Utd academy was overseen by former Irish international and Arsenal star John Devine.

John, now head coach with new League of Ireland club Sporting Fingal, travelled the country to establish Manchester Utd coaching structures at up to fifty schoolboy clubs. In his ten years as United's Director of Coaching in Ireland, John watched as seventy young players who came through the academy went on to professional careers in the game. 'Of those seventy players, fifty-four became international players at different levels, so you can see the huge benefits United's academy has had for Ireland,' John said.

However, he revealed his most satisfying achievement with the academy was the setting up of an All-Ireland team under the United banner. 'We had players from both North and South, such as Jonny Evans and Anthony Stokes, playing in the same team and many of them became great friends,' John said. 'It made me very proud to see that we could work from all corners of Ireland together and I really enjoyed working with Eddie Coulter during the development of the academy.'

George Best celebrates winning the 1968 European Cup.

The Second Busby Era

(1958-1970)

After leading United to the cusp of European glory before disaster struck in 1958, Matt Busby arrived back at the helm of Manchester United more determined than ever to succeed.

He underlined his intentions by guiding a depleted United squad to the runners-up spot in the league in 1959, but fans at Old Trafford knew it was going to take patience for Busby to pull the club back to the top.

Busby began to swell the ranks of the club's youth teams once again, but also made some very clever signings for the first team. Tenacious Irish full-back Noel Cantwell was signed from West Ham in 1960 to add experience to the team and forward David Herd was snapped up from Arsenal a year later. 1961 also heralded the arrival of a twinkle-toed young Irishman with the very apt surname of Best.

Young George was joined at the club by big-money signing Denis Law in 1962, who was lured back from Italian giants Torino for a then British-record transfer fee of £115,000. With Harry Gregg in goal and John Giles, Dennis Viollet and Bobby Charlton also star-ring, Busby was developing the basis for another very successful team.

The first signs of this came in 1963, when Busby led United to the FA Cup final at Wembley where they beat Leicester City 3–1. Noel Cantwell captained the victorious United side that day which also included Irishmen John Giles and Tony Dunne. It heralded the start of Busby's second United revolution which in the years to come would be built around the brilliance of George Best.

Best made his debut on the wing for Manchester United in September 1963 and it marked the beginning of another glorious era in the club's history.

United came within a whisker of winning the First Division title in 1964, eventually finishing second to Liverpool, but with Best, Charlton and Law in full swing, they were not to be denied a year later. United won the

United's players celebrate winning the 1963 FA Cup final.

league on goal difference from Leeds Utd but they were back playing with the swagger that had been such a feature of the original Busby Babes.

They were also back in the European Cup and began the following season's campaign with a devastating 9–2 aggregate victory over HJK Helsinki of Finland. When United followed this up with a 5–1 demolition of Vorwarts Berlin and an even more impressive 8–2 victory over Benfica in the quarter-finals, Red Devils' fans were dreaming of a first ever European Cup final.

However, United just fell short when they lost 2–1 to the talented Yugoslavian side of Partizan Belgrade in the semi-final. It was the third time that Busby had been denied at the semi-final stage, but it seemed only a matter of time before he and United would succeed.

Off the pitch, Old Trafford continued its own transformation.

Club chairman Harold Hardman died in 1965 and was replaced by successful businessman Louis Edwards, who had made his money through a meat packaging business. He had invested in the club in the late 1950s and, by 1965, he had assumed the role of club chairman.

With England due to host the 1966 World Cup, Edwards and the United directors decided to completely redesign the ground's north and east stands.

The ground's old roof pillars were replaced in 1965 with modern-style cantilevering on top of the roof, allowing every spectator a completely unobstructed view. The architects rearranged the organisation of the stands to have terracing at the front and a larger seated area towards the back, as well as the first private boxes at a British football ground.

With the first two stands converted to cantilevers, the club's owners devised a long-term plan to do the same to the other two stands and convert the stadium into a bowl-like arena.

On the pitch, United could only finish fourth in the league in 1966, but when the World Cup was over, there was more to come from Matt Busby's men.

This team – which has also gone down as one of United's best ever – regained the league title in 1967, with young Irishmen Best, Tony Dunne and Shay Brennan as integral members of the team, though injuries and age had taken

A redesigned Old Trafford was one of the venues for the 1966 World Cup.

Matt Busby (right) encourages his players, including Number 7 George Best, as they prepare for extra time in the European Cup final against Benfica at Wembley, 28 May 1968.

their toll on the brilliant Noel Cantwell, whose influence was waning.

The only thing missing for Busby now was a European Cup title and United set about rectifying this in the 1967–68 season.

They started their European Cup campaign with a routine 4–0 victory over Malta's Hibernian, before overcoming the tricky Sarajevo 2–1 to advance once again to the quarter-finals.

United needed all their grit to see off Poland's Gornik Zabrze over two legs to set up a mouth-watering semi-final clash with Real Madrid. The crack Spanish outfit had ruined Busby's European dreams eleven years earlier, but, this time, the canny Scot would exact his revenge.

Leading 1–0 from a George Best goal during the first leg at Old Trafford, United arrived in Madrid confident they could finish off the job and the players put in a heroic performance in Spain to pull off an excellent 3–3 draw, which guaranteed a place in their first ever European Cup final.

On 28 May 1968, United made the short trip to Wembley to take on Portugal's Benfica.

As always, Best, Brennan and Tony Dunne were in the United team that took to the pitch that night. In a tight game that ebbed and flowed, United had to wait until extra time to take control of the match. With the teams tied at 1–1 after ninety minutes, George Best strode forward with an imperious performance in extra time scoring the goal that broke Benfica's hearts as United eventually won 4–1.

It was Matt Busby's greatest triumph as

Frank O'Farrell, Manchester Utd's only Irish manager.

United manager and a fitting way for him and the club to remember the young heroes who had perished in 1958.

Sadly for Busby, this was as good as it would get for Manchester United under his reign.

When United failed to retain their European Cup the following season, and could only finish eleventh in the league, Busby decided to call it a day after twenty-four years of magnificent service to the club. He had led United to five First Division titles and had established himself as one of Britain's greatest managers.

A policeman keeps watch over the Young United fans section at Old Trafford, 1968.

Following his resignation, Busby remained at United as a director of the club, handing over managerial duties to former player Wilf McGuinness.

However, under McGuinness, United only finished eighth in the league in 1970. Following an indifferent start to the next season, he was sacked in December 1970, and Busby was brought back to the helm. He remained there until the end of that season, guiding United to another eighth place finish in the league.

After Irishman Frank O'Farrell took over managerial duties in 1971, Busby reverted to his role as director.

During his twenty-six years as manager, Matt Busby had transformed Manchester United into one of the world football's greatest clubs. He developed two great teams during his tenure and turned United into an institution for fast, skilful and mesmerising football.

By the time he hung up his managerial hat, he had helped Manchester United etch its name into the history of world football. Such was his success, that whoever followed Busby into the Manchester United hot seat was always going to find it next to impossible to emulate his achievements.

As it was, it would be over two decades before United would regain the glory that Busby secured for the club.

Frank O'Farrell

Given the strong connection between Manchester United and Ireland, it was always likely that at some stage the Old Trafford club would come looking for an Irish manager. Perhaps the only surprise is that only once in Manchester United's 130-year history has a man from Ireland run the affairs of the club.

Corkman Frank O'Farrell was entrusted with the job of reigniting the flickering United flame when he took up the post of manager in the summer of 1971. The United team at the time was a pale shadow of the swashbuckling side that had captured the European Cup in 1968. With star player George Best embracing a party lifestyle off the pitch, an ageing United side had failed to replicate their stunning European success and had fallen dramatically into mid-table obscurity by the beginning of the 1970s.

Veteran manager Matt Busby had already attempted to hand over the reins to former United player Wilf McGuinness, but following an unsuccessful stint for the Englishman, Busby again found himself in the managerial seat nearing the end of the 1970–71 season. When that campaign had ended, United left the job of finding Busby's successor up to the Scotsman himself.

After giving it some thought, Busby earmarked Irishman Frank O'Farrell for the job, obviously impressed with his three-year reign with the Foxes, where they had reached the FA Cup final in 1969 and won the Second Division title in May 1971.

At forty-four O'Farrell's managerial career had been on a steady upward spiral. A former inside forward with his hometown club Cork Utd, O'Farrell moved to England in 1948, where he began a successful playing career with West Ham Utd in the Second Division. It was at West Ham that O'Farrell first began to think of becoming a manager.

An enthusiastic student of the game, O'Farrell spent hours talking tactics with his equally dedicated Hammers team-mates Noel Cantwell, Dave Sexton and Malcolm Allison. In 1956, O'Farrell moved from West Ham to play in the First Division with Preston North End, where he continued his football education under the guidance of manager Cliff Britton.

When his playing days were over, O'Farrell, who had also gained nine caps for the Republic of Ireland, cut his teeth in management with non-league Weymouth. From there, he moved on to Fourth Division outfit Torquay Utd in 1965.

During his first season at the club, O'Farrell helped Torquay gain promotion to Division Three, highlighting his motivational and player-management skills. His successful spell at Torquay did not go unnoticed and he turned down a number of attractive offers before deciding to become the manager of Leicester City in December 1968, as the club lay perilously close to the bottom of the First Division table.

Unfortunately, Frank was unable to prevent Leicester's slide out of the First Division that season, but had miraculously managed to bring his ailing team into a much-anticipated FA Cup final with Manchester City in May 1969.

Leicester's impressive Cup run that season had even included an unbelievable 1–0 victory over new English powerhouses Liverpool at their Anfield fortress. O'Farrell's Leicester side were unable to repeat the feat in the final, however, and Manchester City ran out 1–0 winners.

Despite this defeat, Leicester became a force to be reckoned with in the Second Division under O'Farrell, narrowly missing out on promotion in 1970 after finishing third in the table. They made no such mistake the following year, when O'Farrell led Leicester back into the top flight by running away with the Second Division championship. It was this feat, along with O'Farrell's impressive ability to deal with Leicester's big personalities that attracted Busby and United.

O'Farrell had been unwilling to budge when Leicester's up-and-coming star goalkeeper Peter Shilton had agitated for a move away from the club, as he feared playing in the Second Division would ruin his dreams of starring for England. O'Farrell refused to countenance a move, making Shilton get on with the business of playing for Leicester and the young keeper even managed to get his first England call-up whilst playing Second Division football for the Foxes.

This impressed Busby, who knew United needed a strong new manager capable of making the tough decisions which were needed to turn an ageing United side into a real force again.

So, in the summer of 1971, Busby, who had become a director at United, made his move, offering Frank O'Farrell a five-year contract to become the Red Devils' new manager.

Sadly, the Irishman's stint at Old Trafford lasted only eighteen months, ending in a bitter split.

Now happily retired in Torquay in the southwest of England, eighty-one-year-old Frank talks openly about his time at Manchester United, where he firmly believes he was never given a fair crack of the whip.

The affable Corkman was excited to take on one of the biggest jobs in world football, but regretted not being allowed to get on with the job of transforming Manchester United back into the powerful force it had once been. 'Everybody knew Manchester United were on the look out for a new manager in 1971 and while my name had been mentioned with it, I remained indifferent to this speculation. My contract with Leicester City had actually just expired and I was in negotiations with them about signing a new one, so I had no intentions of going anywhere and I never sought the United job. Then I got a phone call from Manchester United to say they were interested in talking to me about taking over as manager from Matt Busby.

'I went to speak to Busby about this and I was naturally very pleased that my work with other clubs had gained me recognition with such a big club. Busby had obviously studied my career as a manager with both Torquay and Leicester and liked what he had seen. He knew I would have some big decisions to make upon becoming United manager and would be dealing with very big players. I know Busby admired the way I had dealt with [the Peter Shilton situation].'

After agreeing the terms of his five-year deal with United, O'Farrell was in no doubt as to just how big a job he had before him. 'United had been on the slide for quite some time before I arrived. Players who should have been moved on after the club had won the European Cup were still there and the team needed to be freshened up. Matt even realised that himself. When he spoke to me about taking the job he said it would take at least three years to turn the club around. I knew myself that the team badly needed some new players and that the guys already there would be looking over their shoulders fearing they could be on their way out. But that is what I had been brought in to do and the start of my time at United proved to be quite successful.'

O'Farrell's introduction to the club certainly seemed to ignite an initial revival in United's fortunes as they started the 1971–72 season with a flourish.

The team lost just once in their first fourteen league games as United opened up an impressive lead at the top of the First Division table. Such had been their dominance in the early part of that season that, in October 1971, Matt Busby announced to the English media that Frank

O'Farrell had been the best signing he had ever made for the club. Much of this initial success had been down to O'Farrell's ability to coax the best out of the irrepressible George Best, who was on fire during the first six months of O'Farrell's reign, scoring goals with ease and helping the team to the summit of the league table.

Frank remembers his time with Best fondly, even if the winger eventually caused him more trouble than he was worth. 'George played absolutely brilliantly for the first six months that I was at the club. The thing about him was that he had also been playing brilliantly in the couple of years leading up to my arrival at United, winning games for the team that they had no right to win. But the team around him had gone backwards significantly and this was a large part of George's frustration.

'When I first came in, George was excellent, even in training, and he would often stay back on the training pitch to put in more practice when the sessions were over. Unfortunately as time went on, George became unreliable and you could not always tell when he was going to turn up or where he would be. He caused me a few headaches over my period as manager as it became difficult to explain to people why George was not around when he was supposed to be. Eventually, in 1972, he went absent without leave altogether and the team simply wasn't the same when he was not in it. I did my best to try and help George and always had his best interests at heart. Despite his problems, which were all off the field, I don't have anything bad to say about George Best. I really liked him as he was a lovely man who could be very funny and, as a footballer, he never did anything but good for me.'

It was in early 1972 when the first problems of O'Farrell's reign began to surface. By the turn of the year, United were still close to the top of the table having lost just twice in twenty-three games, but things soon started to turn sour.

Four successive league defeats in January 1972 turned up the heat on O'Farrell who found his attempts to put his own stamp on the team compromised by Busby's continued presence at the club.

'I knew that some of the players who had been at the club for many years needed to be replaced, but it was very difficult to do anything when Matt was still there in the background, talking to his former players,' Frank stated. 'It was Busby's fault that the team had stagnated in the years following their European Cup success and I had believed it was my job to turn it all

around again. I gave young Sammy McIlroy his first chance in the team and had no problems bringing in new characters such as Scottish defender Martin Buchan from Aberdeen. Martin was a very genuine guy who ended up giving ten years great service to the club and is now remembered as one of United's best defenders. But he was not liked by some of the existing players at the club who were probably finding it difficult to accept the changes that were being made.'

By the end of O'Farrell's first season in charge at Old Trafford, United had finished eighth in the league, but the Irishman was confident of making progress with the team.

During the summer of 1972, O'Farrell brought in forwards Ted McDougall and Trevor Anderson to add to former Notts Forest striker Ian Storie-Moore, who he had bought a few months earlier, and hopes were high that United could launch a serious league title challenge.

Unfortunately for O'Farrell, United made a nightmare start to the new season failing to win in any of their first nine league games. They started the campaign with a 2–1 defeat to Ipswich at Old Trafford and followed this with further losses to Merseyside heavyweights Everton and Liverpool. It wasn't until a 3–0 home victory over Derby County in late September that O'Farrell gained some breathing space. But United still struggled to shake off their malaise and were soon dumped out of the League Cup by lowly Bristol Rovers.

A rare high point for United came in a 2–0 league win over Liverpool at Old Trafford in November 1972, but a home defeat to Stoke City, followed by a 5–0 hammering by Crystal Palace prompted United to act, and O'Farrell was sacked a week before Christmas 1972.

Despite his team's struggles at the time, O'Farrell still finds it difficult to accept how he was dumped so cruelly, only eighteen months into his five-year contract. He still firmly believes that given time, he would have turned the corner with United. 'It was a big job that I had taken on and nobody had been expecting miracles,' he said. 'When Busby first took over at United it took him up to six years to eventually win the league. Everybody knew it was going to take time for me to transform United again and I couldn't understand how Busby could say I had been his best ever signing for the club, yet fifteen months later he was showing me the door. Don't get me wrong, I admire Busby for what he achieved as manager of Manchester United but he was not consistent with everything he said during my time there and did not treat me fairly.

'Even though the team was not playing well around the time I was let go, I knew as a manager

what I had to do and was very confident I would have turned it around. I didn't see any reason why I should have been let go as I had a long time left on my contract and you only have to look at the success which Alex Ferguson gained years after he first became United manager to see how this can happen.'

To add insult to injury, O'Farrell was forced to take legal proceedings to get United to pay up the remaining years of his contract. 'I was legally obliged to sign on the dole after I had left United; the first time I ever had to do that in my life. It was an awful time and it reflected badly on United that such a big club could treat somebody that way. It was a terrible shame as I loved my time at the club and I loved the fans, many of whom supported me during that difficult time.'

Despite this massive setback, Frank has never had any regrets at taking on the role as United manager. 'It was difficult to turn down such an offer as United were such a big club. Leicester City were a very good club in their own right, but Man United had much bigger support and could attract regular gates in excess of 50,000. The potential to achieve great things at United was much bigger than at Leicester and that was why I took on the challenge. The only pity was that Matt Busby obviously still felt that he could have done a better job; if that was the case then he should have stayed on as manager himself instead of appointing me in the first place.'

During his time as a professional footballer and manager, Frank O'Farrell watched many great Irishmen make their name at Manchester United, and while he believes none were better than George Best, a few others still spring to his attention.

'Tony Dunne was an excellent full-back who gave great service to the club. Sammy McIlroy was also very talented and I was delighted to be the first to give him his chance at United. Another great player for United during my playing days was Jackie Carey. I never actually got the chance to play against Jackie during my time with West Ham as the club was stuck in the Second Division, but I did have the honour of playing with him for the Ireland team and it was a marvellous experience.'

Overlooking the bitter end to his time at Old Trafford, Frank still has fond memories of his time in football. 'It was disappointing how it ended but it was only one incident in a whole life-time of football when I developed a very good reputation within the game. In different circumstance and given time, I could very well have enjoyed great success with Manchester United.'

Player Profiles

John Giles	
Place of birth:	Dublin
Date of birth:	6 October 1940
Position:	Midfielder
Years at United:	1957–1963
Games played:	115
Goals:	13
Honours:	FA Cup (1963)

Rated as one of the best players to ever come out of Ireland, Dubliner John Giles arrived at Manchester United at a time when manager Matt Busby was creating one of his greatest teams.

At just sixteen years of age, Giles made the move to Manchester in 1957 to begin a career in football that was to span three decades. During his first year at the club, he spent most of his time playing with the youths, as the all-conquering senior team of Duncan Edwards and a young Bobby Charlton attempted to retain the league title they had won the previous season.

Giles was an outstanding young footballer, able to operate as either winger or inside-forward, but because of the strength of the United team, he was not expected to make the step up to the first team for quite some time.

The following season, Giles was once again playing in the United youth team, but after the Munich Air Disaster in February 1958, he was thrust into the Old Trafford limelight. Shorn of eight first-team players who had died in the disaster, Busby gave Giles his debut against Tottenham in September 1959.

Remarkably, Busby had managed to lead United to second place in the league in 1959, as he began to sow the seeds for a new United revival that Giles now found himself part of.

It was the start of a glittering career for Giles, even if most of it was eventually spent away from United.

Giles also made his debut for the Republic of Ireland at the tender age of eighteen, scoring

Johnny Giles in action against Richie Norman of Leicester in the 1963 FA Cup final.

a cracking goal against Sweden at Dalymount Park.

At Old Trafford, Giles quickly set about establishing himself in the United team, playing mostly in a forward role. He scored his first goal for the club in a 5–0 drubbing of Fulham in March 1960 and added to it with a goal against Arsenal a month later.

Giles' best moment at United came in 1963 when he was part of the team that captured the FA Cup with a 3–1 victory over Leicester City. Indeed, Giles was credited with playing his part in the winning goal with a defence-splitting pass that set up the move which led to David Herd scoring.

United had barely had time to savour their win when Giles, amazingly, put in a transfer request.

He did play in the following season's Charity Shield opener against Everton, but was soon on his way to Leeds Utd in the Second Division for £33,000. Giles would go on to help Leeds enjoy the best fifteen years in the club's history, winning numerous honours.

He also had a remarkable career for the Republic of Ireland, playing for almost two decades before also acting as player-manager in later years.

But, in 1963, Giles had left behind a United team that would go on to win two league titles and a European Cup within five years of his departure.

Other Clubs: Manortown United, Leeds Utd, West Brom
International Record: Republic of Ireland
Caps: 59
Goals: 5

Joseph Carolan	
Place of birth:	Dublin
Date of birth:	8 September 1937
Position:	Defender
Years at United:	1956–1960
Games played:	71
Goals:	0

Full-back Joe Carolan became the latest Irish member of the Matt Busby revolution when he signed for Manchester United from Dublin club Home Farm in February 1956.

At just eighteen, Carolan was young for a defender and spent time building up his game in the United youth team which he had joined when he first arrived. That youth team, which included Bobby Charlton at the time, went on to win the club's fourth FA Youth Cup in a row with victory over Chesterfield in the final.

Whilst Charlton went on to better things in the United first team, Carolan had to wait for his chance.

It wasn't until after the Munich Air Disaster that Carolan was pushed into the United first-team set-up. He made his debut in November 1958 as United beat Luton Town 2–1 at Old Trafford with goals from Charlton and Dennis Viollet.

Carolan became a regular in the team that season and United won the first seven games he was involved in.

His first taste of defeat with United came in the FA Cup, when they were dumped out

by Norwich City after a 3–0 defeat. He played in another fifteen games for United that season, winning eleven, as Matt Busby's side ran Wolves close for the league title.

Carolan remained a key member of United's side for the 1959–60 season, when his old Home Farm club-mate John Giles also became a feature in the team. He played in an impressive forty league games, but United couldn't improve on their previous year's runners-up spot and they finished seventh.

Carolan was part of the United side that enjoyed good FA Cup wins over Derby County and Liverpool, before they bowed out of the competition to Sheffield Wednesday.

He began the 1960–61 season in the United defence when he played in successive defeats to Blackburn and Everton. After this, Busby started to use other options in his squad and Carolan found himself out of the team. He played in just one more match for United, which was a 4–0 League Cup win over Exeter City in October 1960.

After fellow Irishman Noel Cantwell arrived at the club from West Ham in a £29,500 transfer deal in November 1960, Carolan was transferred a month later to Brighton. He left United having played seventy-one games over a three-season period.

Other Clubs: Home Farm, Brighton & Hove Albion
International Record: Republic of Ireland
Caps: 2
Goals: 0

Sammy McMillan	
Place of birth:	Belfast
Date of birth:	20 September 1941
Position:	Forward
Years at United:	1957–1963
Games played:	15
Goals:	6

Sammy McMillan was just sixteen years old when he made the move to Manchester United from the famous Belfast Boyland club in December 1957. He was only weeks into his new adventure when the club was plunged into the most traumatic period of its history with the Munich Air Disaster in February 1958.

McMillan was a member of the United youth team at the time, but every part of the United set-up was affected in some way by the crash.

McMillan continued his progression with the United youth and reserve teams until Matt Busby called him up for first team action in 1961 and the Belfast-born forward made his United debut in November in a side that contained the talents of John Giles, Bobby Charlton and Dennis Viollet.

United were beaten 3–1 by Sheffield Wednesday that day and the team didn't win in any of McMillan's first five games for the club. However, McMillan did show he had a knack for scoring goals when he notched his first for United in a 4–1 defeat to Ipswich Town in only his third game for the first team.

He also showed tremendous pace and the ability to play either on the right, left or in the centre of the forward line.

His next game for United came in April 1962 when he helped himself to another two goals in a 4–3 defeat to Leicester City. His first win for United came in a 5–0 drubbing of Ipswich Town a week later.

McMillan was on the score sheet again as United lost 3–2 to Arsenal at Old Trafford on 16 April, before scoring two more goals in a 3–2 win over Sheffield Utd eight days later.

McMillan played a total of eleven games for United during the 1961–62 season, scoring an impressive six goals but Matt Busby's team finished way down the table in fifteenth place.

Despite having a good scoring ratio, McMillan was finding it difficult to bed down a permanent place in the United first team. He played just four league games for United the following season and failed to score in any of them, and his last game for United was in a 3–0 home defeat to Blackburn Rovers in October 1962.

McMillan remained at Old Trafford for another year before being transferred to Wrexham in an £8,000 deal in December 1963.

He played just twice for Northern Ireland in 1962 against Scotland and England, but the team lost on both occasions.

Other Clubs: Wrexham, Southend, Chester City, Stockport County
International Record: Northern Ireland
Caps: 2
Goals: 0

Harry Gregg	
Place of birth:	Derry
Date of birth:	25 November 1932
Position:	Goalkeeper
Years at United:	1957–1966
Games played:	247
Goals:	0

Of all the heroes who have played for Manchester United down through the years, few have been more deserving of that title than Derry-born goalkeeper Harry Gregg. A survivor of the horrific Munich Air Disaster in 1958 and a goalkeeper of supreme stature

Harry Gregg lies concussed after a heavy challenge from Nat Lofthouse of Bolton in the 1958 FA Cup final.

and skill, Gregg has gone down in history as one of the club's greatest servants.

Signed from Doncaster Rovers by Matt Busby in December 1957, Gregg immediately made the number one position his own in a star-studded United side. He made his debut in a 4–0 drubbing of Leicester City and played his first European Cup game at Old Trafford when United beat Red Star Belgrade 2–1 on 14 January 1958.

He remained between the posts for the return leg, which United drew 3–3, but then came that awful moment when the plane carrying home the victorious team crashed into an icy runway in Munich, killing twenty-three people including eight United players. After surviving the crash himself, Gregg was credited with helping to save the lives of fellow players Bobby Charlton and Dennis Viollet by dragging them out of the plane wreckage.

Incredibly, Gregg was back in the United goal for an emotional FA Cup clash with Sheffield Wednesday just two weeks later, which the Red Devils won 3–0.

A depleted United were eventually dumped out of that season's European Cup by AC Milan and finished eighth in the league, with Gregg in goal for most of the games.

He also helped United reach the FA Cup final in 1958, but it was a game that did not go according to plan for Gregg. The tough keeper was knocked out by Bolton forward Nat Lofthouse as he scored one of his two goals in a 2–0 defeat for United.

Now, firmly established in the United team, and regarded as one of the best goalkeepers in the English First Division, Gregg helped United to second place in the league in 1959. He remained the United custodian through the relatively barren years of 1960–62, as Matt Busby went about building the club back into the force it was before the Munich tragedy.

Things started to look up for United as they went on an FA Cup run in 1963.

Gregg played in goal as United won four FA Cup games on the trot, but he had the misfortune to miss out on his club's final win over Leicester City through injury.

Such bad luck was to dog Gregg throughout the rest of his United career, and injury also prevented him from playing enough games to warrant a league winners' medal when

Harry Gregg.

United claimed the First Division titles in both 1965 and 1967.

On the international front, Gregg played in goal for Northern Ireland on twenty-five occasions in nine years. He made his debut in a 2–1 World Cup qualifier win over Wales in 1954 and featured in all of his country's four games at the World Cup finals in 1958 when they made it as far as the quarter-finals.

His last game for Northern Ireland finished in an 8–3 defeat to England in 1963.

Gregg played his last game for Manchester United against Stoke City in September 1966, the club he was sold to a year later, and so missed out on United's triumphant European Cup campaign in 1968.

By the end of his Old Trafford career, Gregg had played 249 games, keeping forty-eight clean sheets.

Other Clubs: Doncaster Rovers, Stoke City
International Record: Northern Ireland
Caps: 25
Goals: 0

Ronnie Briggs	
Place of birth:	Belfast
Date of birth:	24 March 1943
Position:	Goalkeeper
Years at United:	1958–1964
Games played:	11
Goals:	0

Talented young goalkeeper Ronnie Briggs joined Manchester United straight from school in August 1958, at a time when the club was still trying to recover from the despair of the Munich Air Disaster.

Briggs was only fifteen years old and so spent his time learning the ropes through Matt Busby's excellent youth system and eventually made his full United debut in January 1961.

Unfortunately for him, United were on the wrong end of a 6–0 hammering, making young Briggs' first game for the club one he wanted to forget.

He got over his shaky start to play for the team again just a week later when they drew 1–1 with Sheffield Wednesday in the FA Cup. Misfortune was to dog Briggs in the replay at Old Trafford, however, as a series of errors from him led to United being humbled 7–2 in front of their own crowd.

Manager Matt Busby took Briggs out of the side after that game, and Briggs didn't appear again until just over a year later.

Briggs had better luck in the United goal on his return in February 1962, when the Red Devils defeated West Brom 4–1 and gained a couple of draws with Wolves and Birmingham.

With a keeper of the class of Derryman Harry Gregg already at the club, Briggs' opportunities in the United first team were limited and he played just five more games for United, the highlight of which was a 5–0 win over Ipswich – Briggs' only clean sheet during his time at Old Trafford.

Briggs remained at United throughout 1963 when they won the FA Cup but he was not involved in the campaign.

Matt Busby eventually let Briggs go to Swansea City in 1964, with the goalie having played just eleven games for United. His last match had been in a 3–2 home defeat to Arsenal in April 1962.

Other Clubs: Swansea, Bristol Rovers
International Record: Northern Ireland
Caps: 2
Goals: 0

James Nicholson	
Place of birth:	Belfast
Date of birth:	27 February 1943
Position:	Half-back
Years at United:	1958–1964
Games played:	68
Goals:	6

Half-back Jimmy Nicholson arrived at United aged fifteen in September 1958. He was another in the long line of players from Boyland FC to cross to Manchester, where he hoped to become part of Matt Busby's plans.

Like all Irish youngsters that arrived at United at the time, Nicholson had to wait a few years for his chance in the first team but his opportunity arrived early, when he was still only seventeen.

He made his debut in a 4–0 defeat to Everton in August 1960, but remained in the side that got its own back on their Merseyside rivals just a week later. Nicholson scored his first goal for United in that game, as they beat Everton 4–0 at Old Trafford.

Nicholson cemented his place in the United midfield that season, and appeared in thirty-one league games.

A highlight of the season for Nicholson came at Old Trafford in a 6–0 rout of Chelsea on St Stephen's (Boxing) Day 1960, in which he scored two goals.

Five days later, he was in the United side that hammered Man City 5–1 to finish the year in style.

Nicholson scored one more goal in a 2–1 defeat to Wolves to end his first season in the United team with four goals as they finished in seventh place in the First Division.

Nicholson was in and out of the side at the beginning of the 1961–62 season and didn't score his first goal until a 2–1 FA Cup win over Bolton in January 1962 – which actually proved to be his last goal for the club. He played in seventeen league games that season, as Busby's team finished in the bottom half of the table in fifteenth place.

Busby was beginning to build up the youth section of the club again and was also making significant moves in the transfer market, all of which reduced Nicholson's importance to the team.

85

By Christmas 1962, he had featured in ten of United's league games, but found himself out of the side by the turn of the year.

At the same time, Nicholson had become an important member of the Northern Ireland team, having made his debut back in 1961 against Scotland. Nicholson was sent off in just his third game for his country, which was in a 2–0 World Cup qualifier win over Greece in October 1961. Despite this, he was selected to play for Northern Ireland for a full ten years, scoring six goals during that time.

Nicholson's last game at Old Trafford in early December 1962 had been a happy occasion, as they trounced Notts Forest 5–0.

United would go on to win the FA Cup in 1963 but Nicholson did not feature in any of the games. He remained at the club until December 1964 when he was sold to Huddersfield Town for £8,000.

His last game for United had been a 3–0 defeat away to West Brom on 15 December 1962.

Other Clubs: Huddersfield Town, Bury
International Record: Northern Ireland
Caps: 41
Goals: 6

Noel Cantwell	
Place of birth:	Cork
Date of birth:	28 February 1932
Position:	Left full-back
Years at United:	1960-1967
Games played:	146
Goals:	8
Honours:	First Division (1965, 1967); FA Cup (1963)

Noel Cantwell signed for Manchester United in 1960, after eight great years with West Ham, and went on to become one of the Red Devils' most inspirational players of the 1960s.

Matt Busby shelled out £29,500 for left-back Cantwell, which was a record for any full-back at the time. However, the cunning United coach got great value for his money, as the honest and elegant Corkman helped his new club back to the very top in the English game.

Noel Cantwell tackles
Jimmy Greaves in the
1962 FA Cup semi-final.

He was an interesting character who had even played international cricket for Ireland before embarking on a career in professional football. His experience meant he became a vital part of Busby's new-look United side.

Cantwell's debut for United in November 1960 didn't go so well, however, as they lost 3–0 to Cardiff. But with his Irish international team-mate Shay Brennan playing on the other side of defence, United won seven of the next eight games that Cantwell played in as they showed early signs of things to come.

Cantwell's first goal for United came in a 3–0 win over Middlesbrough in an FA Cup tie at Old Trafford in January 1961. A month later, he was in the United side that was unceremoniously dumped out of the Cup by Sheffield Wednesday in a 7–2 replay defeat.

Cantwell would have to wait two years before enjoying better times in the FA Cup with United, when he captained the team that captured the Cup for the first time in fifteen years in 1963.

That Cup win heralded the beginning of a new glorious era for United under Busby, and Cantwell was in the thick of the action. A player who always demanded respect from fellow professionals for his whole-hearted displays, it was no surprise that Busby made Cantwell club captain.

Cantwell also had the honour of captaining the Republic of Ireland on twenty-two occasions, including a game at Wembley against England. He was used in a number of various roles for the Irish side, including as a forward, and he scored thirteen goals during his thirty-six international appearances.

In 1963, he was playing in the same United side as Denis Law, Bobby Charlton and John Giles and a lot more was now expected of this talented side. As it was, United struggled terribly in the league that year, and they narrowly escaped relegation, finishing fourth from bottom.

Cantwell's United were a different proposition in the FA Cup, however, as they waltzed through to a Wembley final date with Leicester City – Aston Villa were the only top-flight team United had encountered before playing Leicester in the final.

Cantwell and Giles both played that day, as the Red Devils won 3–1, giving the Corkman the honour of climbing the famous Wembley steps to receive the cup in front of delirious United fans.

Cantwell remained United captain for the 1963–64 season, as the team showed significant improvements in their league form to finish runners-up to Liverpool. United also made a determined challenge to hold on to the FA Cup. Cantwell was in the side that coasted past Bristol Rovers and Barnsley before needing three games to overcome Sunderland in the quarter-finals. That win set up an exciting semi-final clash with a talented West Ham team, but Cantwell's hopes of lifting the FA Cup again were dashed in a 3–1 defeat, as his old club went on to win the Cup that year.

United put this disappointment behind them and went on to win the league the following year, but Cantwell missed almost all of it through injury.

The United club captain just made it back in time to enjoy crucial league wins over

Cantwell lifts the FA Cup, 1963.

Birmingham and Liverpool, as the Red Devils captured the league from Leeds Utd on goal difference.

In a cruel twist, mounting injuries also meant the ageing Cantwell was out of the United side for most of the 1966–67 season when they recaptured the league. His final match for United came in a 2–1 victory over Southampton in November 1966 as United marched on to the league title.

It was the full-back's misfortune that United's successful European Cup campaign of 1968 came just a couple of years too late. Nevertheless, Noel Cantwell will go down as one of Matt Busby's shrewdest signings. He brought a professionalism and experience that was badly needed to a United team still shaken from the aftermath of Munich.

Noel Cantwell died on 8 September 2005, at the age of seventy-three.

Other Clubs: Cork Athletic, West Ham
International Record: Republic of Ireland
Caps: 36
Goals: 13

Shay Brennan	
Place of birth:	Manchester
Date of birth:	6 June 1937
Position:	Full-back
Years at United:	1955–1970
Games played:	359
Goals:	6
Honours:	First Division (1965, 1967); European Cup (1968)

Local lad Shay Brennan signed as a youth player for Manchester United in 1955. Although born in Manchester, he was the son of Irish parents and would go on to be a full Republic of Ireland international.

Brennan's first role at the club was to help the youth team win its third FA Youth Cup in a row in 1955.

With Matt Busby's United team conquering all before them, Brennan had to wait patiently for his chance in the first team. When it did arrive, it was unfortunately due to the tragic events of the Munich Air Disaster.

When United returned to action just a fortnight after the fatal tragedy, Brennan was thrust into the side as an inside-left in the FA Cup game against Sheffield Wednesday. He could hardly have made a more dramatic introduction, scoring two goals in a 3–0 United win.

Brennan also starred in the semi-final of the FA Cup that year, scoring again as United beat Fulham 5–3 in a replay. Unfortunately for him, he did not feature in the final, and United were beaten 2–0 by Bolton.

Brennan started the 1958–59 season as a right-back and remained there for the best part of the next eleven years, enjoying some of the most glorious moments in the club's history.

He became an extremely popular figure amongst United fans with his tough and honest displays in a red shirt. He was strong in the tackle and his hard work allowed the midfielders in front of him to play attractive football. Brennan was also a skilful player with great positional sense and he was a hugely important member of United's defence as Matt Busby created his second great team.

Brennan had the misfortune of missing out on a second FA Cup final in 1963.

Despite playing the four games leading up to the final, Brennan missed United's 3–1 win over Leicester City, after Busby chose to play Cantwell and Tony Dunne in the full-back positions. However, he resumed his place in the team to help United clinch their fourth league title under Busby in 1965. Brennan was a virtual ever-present in the team that year that also included fellow Irishmen Tony Dunne, George Best and Noel Cantwell.

In 1965, Brennan also became the first player born outside of Ireland to be capped by the Republic of Ireland. He would go on to play nineteen times for the Irish team and was captain for four of those games.

Brennan's impeccable consistency meant he was still a key member of the United team that won the league again in 1967, playing a brand of football far superior to any other team in England at the time.

His greatest moment on a football field came a year later at Wembley, when a George Best-inspired United clinched the European Cup with a 4–1 victory over Benfica.

This was the last major honour Brennan won with United as the Red Devils failed to reach the heights of their fantastic European Cup win again during his time at the club.

Brennan's last game for United came in January 1970, under Wilf McGuinness, in a 1–0 FA Cup win over Ipswich Town.

Shay Brennan passed away in Waterford on 9 June 2000, the first member of the 1968 European Cup winning team to die. During his funeral, loyal Brennan's coffin was decked out in his Irish, Manchester United and Waterford colours.

Other Clubs: Waterford Utd
International Record: Republic of Ireland
Caps: 19
Goals: 0

91

Tony Dunne	
Place of birth:	Dublin
Date of birth:	24 July 1941
Position:	Left-back
Years at United:	1960–1973
Games played:	535
Goals:	2
Honours:	First Division (1965, 1967); FA Cup (1963); European Cup (1968)

After helping his club Shelbourne to win the FAI Cup in May 1960, full-back Tony Dunne was bought by manager Matt Busby for £5,000. The deal turned out to be one of the best pieces of business Busby ever did as the tenacious Dunne went on to be one of United's greatest servants.

Whilst he played mainly at left-back, Dunne was equally comfortable playing on the right side of defence and it didn't take him too long to nail down a place in the first team. He made his debut against Burnley in October 1960 in a game that produced no less than eight goals, as United suffered a 5–3 defeat.

Busby was careful not to introduce Dunne

Tony Dunne going in for the tackle against Bryan Douglas of Blackburn, 1964.

to the team too soon and he appeared in just four more games for United that season as he settled in to his new surroundings.

Dunne got his first chance for an extended run in the team at the beginning of the 1961–62 season because of an injury to his fellow countryman, and club captain, Noel Cantwell. Dunne seized the opportunity with both hands and impressed Busby so much with his pace and excellent tackling that Cantwell struggled to get back into the team when he returned from his injury.

Dunne played in twenty-eight league games for United that season as he established himself as a regular in the team at just twenty years of age.

The young full-back continued his progression at United when he played in twenty-five league games the following season and also helped United to reach the FA Cup final. He was also in the United team that accounted for Coventry and Southampton on their way to a Cup final date with Leicester City.

Dunne joined Noel Cantwell and John Giles for the final when United beat Leicester 3–1 to claim the first piece of silverware for

United since before the Munich Air Disaster in 1958.

Dunne was also an excellent servant to the Republic of Ireland team and played thirty-three games for his country over a thirteen-year period from 1962.

Dunne's remarkable consistency as either a left- or right-back ensured he was ever present in the United team for the next two years as the team prepared to launch an assault on the First Division title in 1965. He played in every single one of United's forty-two league games during the 1964–65 season as the club claimed back the league title they had last won under Matt Busby in 1957.

The 1965–66 season is notable for the fact that Dunne managed to score his first goal for United in a 3–3 draw with West Brom in an end-of-season game.

Unfortunately, United were unable to claim any silverware that season, but Dunne was back for more the following year. He played in forty of United's forty-two games in the next campaign as the Red Devils won their second league title in three seasons.

United were now ready for an assault on the European Cup and Dunne, as always, was there to help them out. He played in every game as United marched on to a semi-final clash with Real Madrid, which, after a titanic tussle, United won 4–3 on aggregate.

The highlight of Dunne's career came in the European Cup final in May 1968 when he played his part to help United overcome Benfica 4–1 after extra time in an historic occasion at Wembley. Though it would probably have been hard for him to believe then

that it would be the last medal he would win at United, even though he stayed on at the club for another five years.

In the 1968–69 season, Dunne appeared in the United side that travelled to Ireland for a European Cup game against Waterford Utd in September 1968. The Red Devils were clear favourites to win the game and they did just that with a hat-trick from the lethal Denis Law in a 3–1 win.

Dunne missed both ties in the semi-final against AC Milan through injury, but United were defeated 2–1 on aggregate and were unable to hold on to their European crown.

Despite the change in manager to Wilf McGuinness, Dunne's consistency never wavered and he returned to the team, though United failed to reach the heights gained

under Busby. Dunne had remained an excellent member of the team throughout the time McGuinness was manager, playing in over sixty games during his tenure.

When Irishman Frank O'Farrell took over as manager for the 1971–72 season, Dunne remained United's first choice at left-back. He played in thirty-four league games that season but United continued to struggle, and finished only eighth in the league.

Dunne was soon playing for his fourth manager at United when Scotsman Tommy Docherty was brought into the club midway through the 1972–73 season. However, Docherty was not a fan of Dunne's and played him in only four matches for the rest of that season. Dunne's last game for United was in a 4–1 loss to Ipswich on 17 February 1973.

That summer, he was allowed to leave United for Second Division Bolton Wanderers on a free transfer. During his thirteen years at the Old Trafford, Tony Dunne had played in a phenomenal 535 games. To this day, he remains in the top ten for most player appearances for Manchester United.

Other Clubs: Shelbourne, Bolton Wanderers, Detroit Express
International Record: Republic of Ireland
Caps: 33
Goals: 0

Pat Dunne	
Place of birth:	Dublin
Date of birth:	9 February 1943
Position:	Goalkeeper
Years at United:	1964–1967
Games played:	67
Goals:	0
Honours:	First Division (1965)

After starring in goal for the all-conquering Shamrock Rovers side of the early 1960s, Dublin-born goalkeeper Pat Dunne joined Manchester United in May 1964 when Matt Busby paid £10,500 for him. It was money well spent as Dunne helped the team to their first league title in eight years.

Dunne's arrival at Old Trafford couldn't have been better timed, as United's goalkeeper Harry Gregg was being dogged by persistent injuries. It meant Dunne fitted straight in to the United team from the beginning of the 1964–65 season and he went about his business with the minimum of fuss.

There was a huge buzz around the United team that year, due in no small way to the arrival of wonder-boy George Best, and the team remained unbeaten in the first nineteen games that Dunne kept goal for them.

United even embarked on an exciting European Fairs Cup run that season, before bowing out to crack Hungarian side Ferencvarosi TC in the semi-finals.

By the end of his first season, Dunne had helped United to clinch the league title on goal difference from Leeds Utd – with an

Pat Dunne saves against Tottenham Hotspur, 1964.

impressive seventeen clean sheets in thirty-seven league games.

Dunne remained United's number one at the beginning of the 1965–66 season when they got their new campaign up and running with a 2–2 draw with Liverpool in the Charity Shield. However, he soon found his position under threat from the returning Gregg and fellow keeper John Gaskell.

As Busby rotated the three keepers, Dunne played in only eight games that season as they lost their grip on the league title to Liverpool.

Dunne played in two of United's European Cup games that year, keeping a clean sheet in the 6–0 rout of HJK Helsinki at Old Trafford and letting just the one goal past as United also beat German side ASK Vorwaerts 3–1. United marched on to a semi-final date with Partizan Belgrade in 1966 but Dunne lost his place in goal to Gregg.

Dunne remained at United for the beginning of the following season but was soon on his way out of the club as Busby splashed out £55,000 on Chelsea goalkeeper Alex Stepney. Dunne's last game for the club was a 5–1 League Cup defeat to Blackpool on 14 September 1966.

In February 1967, Dunne was sold to Plymouth Argyle for £5,000. During his three years at United, he had played in sixty-seven games and kept twenty-five clean sheets.

Other Clubs: Stella Maris, Everton, Shamrock Rovers, Plymouth Argyle
International Record: Republic of Ireland
Caps: 5
Goals: 0

When Manchester Utd Played in Ireland

Waterford Utd 1–3 Manchester Utd

European Cup

Lansdowne Road, 2 October 1968

Just four months after winning the European Cup, Matt Busby's Manchester Utd side began the defence of their title in Ireland after being paired with Waterford Utd in a first-round tie.

As with the game against Shamrock Rovers a decade earlier, Man Utd mania gripped the nation as Irish fans got ready to greet their heroes in the flesh.

Such was the popularity of United in Ireland, that the game was transferred from Waterford's home ground, Kilcohan Park, to Lansdowne Road in Dublin, which could accommodate a crowd of up to 50,000. It was the first soccer match to be played at the fabled rugby ground in over forty years – since an Irish Free State team had entertained Italy in 1926.

The pitch was in excellent condition for the arrival of Busby's superstars, who were expecting a tough challenge from the League of Ireland champions. Speaking before the game, Busby complemented the strength of the Waterford side, claiming them to be the best football team to come out of the Republic of Ireland since the Shamrock Rovers team of the mid-1950s.

Waterford manager Vinnie Maguire played down his side's chances of causing a huge upset, however, stating that they would have to play ten times better than normal to have any chance of beating United.

Some hope for Waterford came in the form of the indifferent start United had made to their league campaign in England, where their defence was shipping a lot of goals – they had conceded nine goals in just two games, losing 4–0 to Chelsea and 5–4 to Sheffield Utd.

But Waterford manager Maguire made the shock decision to leave out his top centre-forward Phil Buck – a summer signing from

Oxford Utd – in favour of starting with John O'Neill and Seamus Coad up front.

Busby started with all his top stars on the pitch, including mercurial winger George Best and lethal striker Denis Law. Best's presence alone ensured there was a bumper crowd at Lansdowne before kick off, with hundreds of fans scaling walls and risking injury on barbed wire to get into the game. The official attendance was estimated at 48,000, but many more had made it into the ground, with fans almost spilling out onto the pitch.

When the game finally kicked off, Waterford started brightly and had United under pressure with a swift move early on. The magnificent Waterford inside-right Alfie Hale connected with a cross from John O'Neill that United defender Billy Foulkes was happy to deflect out for a corner.

That early scare jolted United into action and it wasn't long before they had breached the Waterford rearguard.

Inevitably, George Best was involved as he evaded the tackle of Vinnie Maguire on the right wing to slip a ball through to Denis Law, who used his strength to brush off the tackle from Jackie Morley to send a shot past Peter Thomas in the Waterford goal.

Thomas had managed to get a hand to Law's shot but this was not enough to stop it from ending up in the net. With just eight minutes on the clock, Waterford were behind and already facing an uphill battle.

The early goal meant United could play the game cleverly, as David Sadler sat deep in front of the defence, with Bobby Charlton also operating in a deeper role.

Further forward, Best and Law were giving Waterford defenders Jimmy McGeough and Noel Griffin a torrid time whenever they got on the ball. Best, in particular, was treating the huge Lansdowne crowd to a virtuoso performance as he teased the Waterford defence at every opportunity.

The ground erupted in the twenty-fourth minute after Best collected a pass from Sadler to swivel in the box and send a beautiful shot into the top corner of the net. Best was mobbed by hordes of adoring fans who had run onto the pitch to celebrate his goal. However, their delight was short lived as the goal was cruelly ruled out by the referee for an offside on United striker Brian Kidd.

It was a major let-off for Waterford, who were finding it difficult to impose themselves on the game.

United goalkeeper Alex Stepney had just three shots to deal with in the entire first half, the best of which came from the irrepressible Hale on thirty-seven minutes.

After a brief lull in their own attacking prowess, United picked things up again just before half-time to score a killer second goal. Law was again the scorer as he rose majestically in the box on forty minutes to head home a free kick from Kidd.

If Waterford had hoped for an easier second half, they were to be badly disappointed as Best continued to torment.

On fifty-three minutes, he dispossessed Maguire down the right to set up Law who flicked the ball home for his third goal. Law's brilliant hat-trick was met with hysteria from the crowd and, similar to Best in the first half, he was mobbed by fans. Busby later remarked how incredible it was for an 'away' team to be greeted with such affection from the home crowd.

Refusing to give up on the game, Waterford fought bravely to put United on the back foot and were rewarded for their efforts in the sixty-fifth minute when John Matthews scored to set up a thrilling last quarter to the game.

Matthews responded quickest in the box after a Casey shot had been blocked, and beat Rimmer in the United goal, who had replaced the injured Alex Stepney. The goal lifted the Waterford fans who mobbed Matthews.

The home side should have added a second late on in the game when Alfie Hale, who never stopped running all night, was unlucky to see his header crash back off the crossbar in the eighty-fifth minute. It proved to be Waterford's last chance as United hung on for a 3–1 win. Busby complemented the Waterford team on the tough game afterwards, saying that they had all impressed him.

The return leg at Old Trafford a fortnight later was an altogether different affair as United ran out easy 7–1 winners, to cap off a 10–2 aggregate victory.

United marched on to the semi-finals of the European Cup that year, before losing 2–1 on aggregate to the eventual champions AC Milan.

REFEREE: W.J. Mullan (Scotland)

ATTENDANCE: 48,000

Waterford United

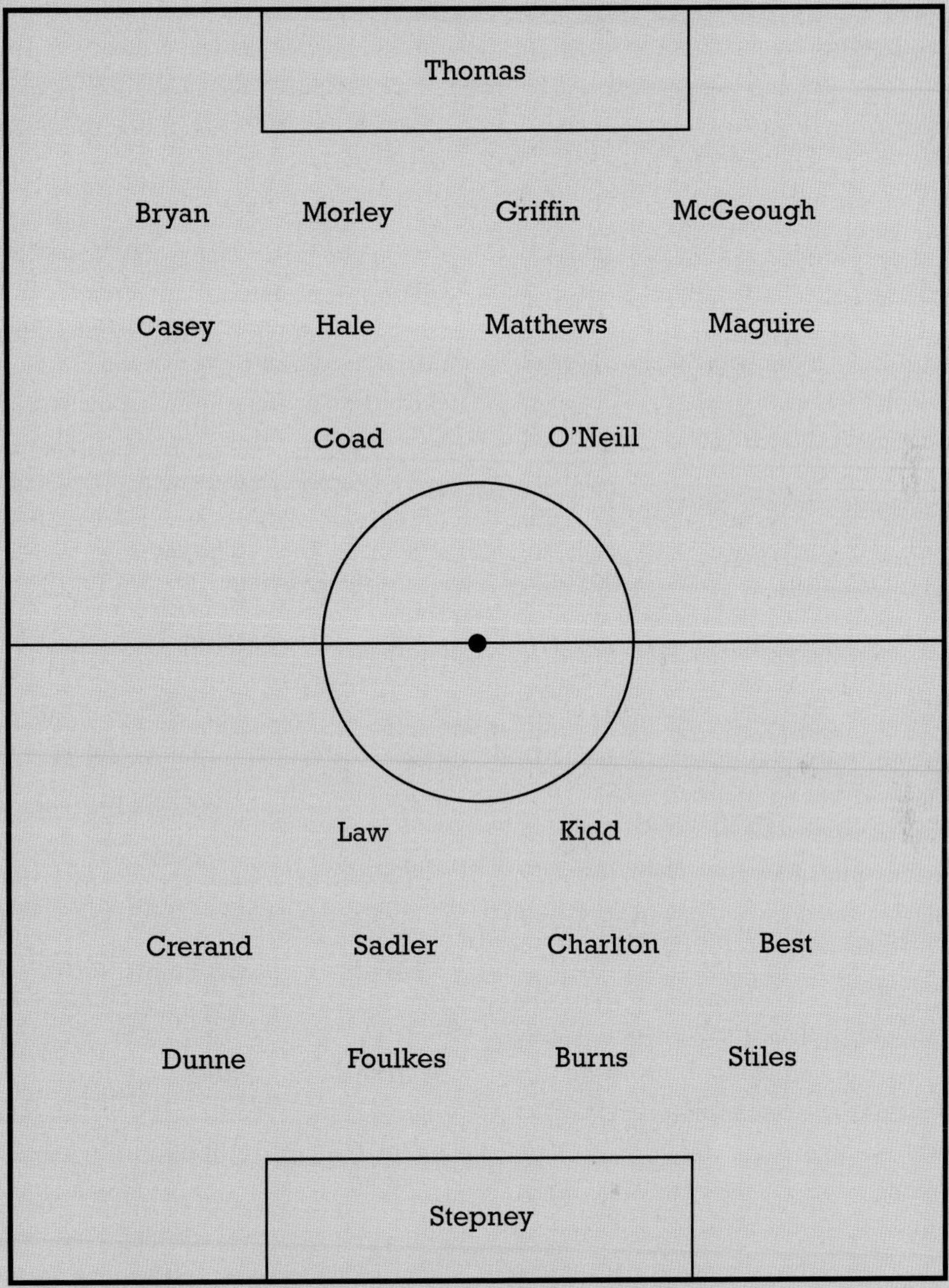
Thomas
Bryan
Morley
Griffin
McGeough
Casey
Hale
Matthews
Maguire
Coad
O'Neill
Law
Kidd
Crerand
Sadler
Charlton
Best
Dunne
Foulkes
Burns
Stiles
Stepney

Manchester United

George Best	
Place of birth:	Belfast
Date of birth:	22 May 1946
Position:	Winger
Years at United:	1962–1974
Games played:	470
Goals:	179
Honours:	First Division
	(1965, 1967);
	European Cup (1968)

Before George Best had even arrived at Manchester United, he was being described as a genius. United's top Northern Ireland scout Bob Bishop had laid eyes on Best playing for his local club Cregagh Boys and wasted no time in advising Matt Busby to snap him up. Best was on his way to Old Trafford as a sixteen-year-old apprentice in 1961.

Best impressed Busby so much that he was in the United first team within two years, making his debut in a 1–0 win over West Brom in September 1963. Busby was careful to protect young Best, however, and didn't play him again until three months later during a league game at Old Trafford against Burnley when Best scored in a 5–1 romp for United, kick-starting his exciting Old Trafford career.

Playing either on the wing or up front, Best terrorised teams all over the country as defenders just couldn't work out how to stop him. Blessed with tremendous pace and strength, he could play equally well with either foot and also had excellent heading ability. There was little Best couldn't do with a ball at his feet and when he didn't have it, he would work just as hard to win it back.

Best became the central figure around whom Busby built his second great United team.

He helped United finish in second place in the league in 1964, scoring six goals in his debut season. The United fans had warmed to Best throughout the 1963–64 season as they realised they had a true footballing great playing in their side. Over the next four years, he would treat them to some of the best football moments of their lives.

The following season – which was his first full campaign – saw Best win his first medal as United lifted the League Championship on goal difference from fierce rivals Leeds Utd. Best played in the majority of United's league games that year as he built up a lethal understanding with Bobby Charlton and Denis Law.

He started the following season by scoring at Wembley as United drew 2–2 with Liverpool in the Charity Shield.

Many of Best's better performances that year for United came in the European Cup, when the rest of the continent got to know about this rising young star. He scored two goals as United hammered HJK Helsinki 6–0 at Old Trafford and also helped United ease past German side ASK Voerwerts 5–1 on their way to a meeting with famed Portuguese side Benfica in the quarter-finals.

United won the first leg at Old Trafford 3–2, but Best's performance in the second leg

George Best.

Bobby Charlton congratulates George Best on one of his goals for United, 1971.

in Portugal has gone down as one of his greatest ever. He ran rings around the Benfica defence that night, scoring two goals and assisting in others as United romped to an unexpected 5–1 win.

Best's reputation was growing both on and off the pitch and his increasing fame and flamboyant nature led many to regard him as

football's first great superstar – he was even dubbed the 'fifth Beatle'.

On the field of play, Best continued to dazzle as he helped United to another league crown in 1967. At just twenty-one, he had already won two league championship medals and he looked to have a career laden with glory still ahead of him.

United began the 1967–68 season with the European Cup firmly in their sights. Best played his part as a goal at Old Trafford helped them to squeeze past Sarajevo in the second round, as Busby's team eyed up a route to the final. However, standing in United's way in the semi-final was the imperious Real Madrid.

The Spanish giants had been the kings of Europe for many years, winning more European Cups than any other side. Best took all this in his stride as he scored the winning goal at Old Trafford to help United to a 1–0 first-leg win.

After United put in a heroic performance in Spain to draw 3–3, the stage was set for Best to show the world what he could do in the European Cup final against Benfica at Wembley.

The Belfast-born winger proved his brilliance in the final, when he inspired United to a 4–1 extra-time win over their Portuguese opponents. Best scored a magnificent goal to put United ahead 2–1 in the game and his performance in extra time was the main reason United had won their first ever European Cup.

He finished the season as United's top scorer with thirty-two goals in all competitions and was also deservedly named both the English and European Footballer of the Year.

Best had reached the pinnacle of club football at just twenty-two, but, tragically, the European Cup win would be the last major honour of his career.

Although United may not have won another trophy during his time there, Best continued to be their star player. He maintained his rich vein of goal scoring with a total of twenty-two goals in all competitions in the 1968–69 season and the following three seasons were similarly prolific. He found the net twenty-two times in the 1969–70 campaign and the next two seasons brought hauls of twenty-two and twenty-seven goals respectively.

He was United's top league scorer in those four seasons and even managed to score six goals in an 8–2 FA Cup win over Northampton in 1970 – the most goals scored by one player in a single game in England.

But off the field, Best was being distracted by his growing 'pop star' lifestyle.

After Matt Busby departed as manager,

> ## 'If I'd been ugly, you'd have never heard of Pele.'
>
> *A modest George Best, explaining his biggest downfall as a footballer.*

George Best celebrates his goal against Benfica, to give United a 2–1 lead in the European Cup final, 1968.

successive United managers Frank O'Farrell and Tommy Docherty found it difficult to keep Best in check, as the player's drinking and partying spiralled out of control.

United had also suffered a drastic downturn in fortunes since conquering Europe in 1968 and Best had become frustrated at their inability to remain as the top club in English football.

Best's hectic lifestyle saw his performances and fitness levels suffer and, after just twelve appearances in the 1973–74 season, he ended his United career. He played his last game for the club in a 3–0 defeat against Queens Park Rangers on New Year's Day 1974 at just twenty-seven years of age.

During his football career, Best had also played thirty-seven times for Northern Ireland but, unfortunately, never got the opportunity to showcase his skills at a major finals event. By the time Northern Ireland had qualified for the World Cup in 1982, the thirty-six-year-old winger's best days were well behind him.

Despite his early departure from United, Best had still managed to play in a phenomenal 470 games for the club.

The mercurial winger has gone down in history as the most naturally gifted player to have played for United, and possibly the best the world has ever seen. He continued to play football for teams as far and wide as America and Ireland, but he was never able to repeat the heroics of his early United years.

When his career was over, Best's drinking continued and it took a huge toll on his health and he died on 5 November 2005, at the age of fifty-nine.

His funeral in Belfast on 3 December 2005, attracted 100,000 people who came to say goodbye to Northern Ireland's greatest sporting hero.

Other Clubs: Dunstable Town, Stockport County, Cork Celtic, LA Aztecs, Fulham, Fort Lauderdale Strikers, Hibernian, San Jose Earthquakes, Bournemouth, Brisbane Lions, Tobermore Utd
International Record: Northern Ireland
Caps: 37
Goals: 9

Don Givens	
Place of birth:	Limerick
Date of birth:	9 August 1949
Position:	Striker
Years at United:	1966–1970
Games played:	9
Goals:	1

A young Don Givens arrived at Old Trafford in September 1965, just as Matt Busby was forming his second great Manchester Utd team. A fresh-faced sixteen-year-old, Givens had been scoring goals for Dublin Rangers before making the move to Manchester where he had signed on as a trainee.

In December 1966, Givens signed his first professional contract with United and it was during his first season as a professional with

Don Givens heads for goal against West Brom, 1969.

the club, that United clinched their second First Division title in three years by playing some scintillating football.

Givens was not yet part of the first-team set-up, however, as Busby still called on the talents of the magnificent George Best, Denis Law and Bobby Charlton. That trio was central to United's historic first European Cup triumph in 1968, when Givens was still only on the periphery of the team.

Busby eventually gave Givens his United debut in August 1969 in a 2–2 draw away to Crystal Palace. Givens remained part of the first team squad for the majority of that season, when he played in another seven league games and one League Cup tie, scoring just one goal in a 3–1 win over Sunderland.

But United were no longer the force they had been just two years earlier and they slipped dramatically that season to finish only eighth in the league as Everton were crowned champions.

Givens had actually been sold before the season's end, when he was transferred to Luton Town in April for £15,000. He spent two years at Luton, before joining up with future United manager Dave Sexton at Queens Park Rangers. Givens enjoyed six great years at QPR, scoring over eighty goals for the club and narrowly missing out on a First Division league title by one point to Liverpool in 1976.

Givens also enjoyed an excellent twelve-year international career with the Republic of Ireland, scoring nineteen goals, including a memorable hat-trick against the powerful USSR in 1974.

Don Givens is still heavily involved in football in Ireland, where he is manager of the Irish Under-21 football team.

Other Clubs: Luton Town, Queens Park Rangers, Birmingham City, Bournemouth, Sheffield Utd, Neuchatel Xamax
International Record: Republic of Ireland
Caps: 56
Goals: 19

Bertie Ahern

"I first heard of Manchester United when my father brought me to the funeral of Liam Whelan in February 1958 following the Munich Air Disaster.

Prior to this, I would have had little knowledge of the club as I was only six-and-a-half years old at the time. I can recall that the funeral cortege stopped outside the ground of Liam Whelan's former club Home Farm and my father explained to me about the huge tragedy of what had happened. From then on, I took a close interest in Manchester United, first listening out for their results on the radio or in the papers.

It was, therefore, a great honour for me that, exactly fifty years after those events, I had the pleasure of laying a wreath in memory of Liam Whelan during a Munich memorial service in Cabra on 6 February 2008.

One of my most enjoyable memories of supporting Man Utd as a young lad was watching Noel Cantwell captain the team that won the 1963 FA Cup final against Leicester. We wouldn't have had television for very long back then, possibly only for about a year, so it was a great thrill to see the game on TV. The fact that Cantwell was from Cork made it even more special, as both my parents were from there. He was my first big hero at Man Utd.

By the age of twelve, I was making trips over to Old Trafford with my Home Farm club and team-mates to watch United play, and we would sometimes even head down to the training ground to watch the team prepare for games. The mid-1960s was a great time to be supporting Man Utd as they had a very good team and George Best had burst onto the scene.

United won the league a couple of times around then and set off on their great European Cup run in 1967–68. I can remember watching the final against Benfica with some of my mates back home and it was a brilliant achievement for the team to win that night.

The following season, I was in the crowd at Lansdowne Road when United came to Ireland to take on Waterford in the European Cup. Waterford were a very good team at the time and they attracted large crowds to their games. But the fact the game had been moved to Lansdowne

Road proved a big novelty, as no football matches had been played there in a long time. United played well that night and when Denis Law completed his hat-trick in a 3–1 win, he was mobbed by all the Irish fans at the game.

This took the United players and management by surprise as they hadn't quite realised just how popular they were in Ireland. I think they thought we just kept an interest in the Irish players who played on the team, but from then on they realised just how big a support base they had over here.

The United team that played that night were a very good side and they had their fair share of Irish guys in the team, including Best, Shay Brennan and Tony Dunne.

Things weren't so good for United throughout the 1970s and 1980s when Liverpool came onto the scene in a big way. We went an awful long time without winning the league and, at times, it looked as if Liverpool were unbeatable.

A group of us had made the habit of going over to Old Trafford for United's last home game of the season, and each year we would be asking ourselves if we would ever get to see the team win the league again.

It was particularly bad in 1992 when they just lost out to Leeds and, after twenty-six years, we began to think it was just never going to happen. So, you can imagine the elation when United finally managed to win the Premier League in 1993 and everything has turned from there.

I believe a player who had a massive influence on this was Eric Cantona.

We all know George Best was a brilliant player who was capable of turning a game at any moment and Cantona could do this too. United won a couple of league titles in the mid-1990s which were down to single goal winners Cantona scored in big games when it really mattered.

When you talk about what makes a genius in football, I think it is the player who can win or turn games on his own, and Cantona was one guy who could do this.

The way Alex Ferguson transformed the fortunes of the club has also been amazing.

I have been lucky enough since as far back as my time as Lord Mayor of Dublin to get to know Alex, and he is a real gentleman. He even brought his team over to visit the sick children in Temple Street Hospital one year and he has a great interest in Irish history, particularly in James Connolly.

I think he brought huge professionalism to the club.

One thing I have always admired about Manchester United is just how professional they are at going about their business. If something goes wrong one week, they just work harder to make sure they get it right the next week, which is very inspirational.

For sheer excitement, the best game United were ever involved in was the 1999 Champions League final with Bayern Munich. I had been over to watch the team play in the quarter- and semi-finals that year but decided to remain at home for the final and it is hard to imagine a more exciting way they could have won than by scoring two goals in the final minute.

There have been some heartbreaking moments supporting United too, and the saddest occasion had to be when Denis Law scored a goal for Manchester City that relegated United to the Second Division in 1974. That was really hard to take as Law had been such a hero for United before that.

What makes me very proud to be a Manchester United fan is the affection that the club holds for Ireland. The Irish Tricolour flag flies over Old Trafford and there is a special connection between this country and United that is every bit as strong as Ireland's connection with Glasgow Celtic.

You couldn't ask for your country to be respected by a top Premiership team any more than having it fly your flag over its stadium. 〞

*Norman Whiteside congratulates
Kevin Moran, 1985.*

Post-Busby United

(1971-1986)

With Manchester United's players, directors and fans finally having to accept the departure of Matt Busby from the position of manager, Irishman Frank O'Farrell bravely stepped into the breach in 1971.

O'Farrell had just guided Leicester City to the Second Division title in style, but he had a massive job on his hands at Old Trafford.

Apart from working in the shadow of Busby's phenomenal achievements, Corkman O'Farrell also had to deal with an increasingly wayward George Best and an ageing side in turmoil. Despite this, O'Farrell's first season started very well and United were even ten points clear at the top of the table at one stage. However, things soon began to unravel and O'Farrell struggled to keep United on track as they fell away to finish back in eighth place at the end of the 1971–72 season.

In a bid to halt United's alarming slide in form, O'Farrell splashed big money on Aberdeen defender Martin Buchan and Nottingham Forest striker Ian Storie Moore, but this did little to prevent a poor start to United's new season and O'Farrell found himself ousted from the manager's position by December 1972.

It meant that after two decades of having just the one manager in charge, United were looking for their fourth manager in less than four years.

Scotsman Tommy Docherty was chosen to succeed O'Farrell and his confident no-nonsense style made him an instant hit with the fans. Unfortunately for Docherty, he was faced with the same problems that had dogged O'Farrell.

As United's all-conquering side of the mid-1960s aged, new-look Liverpool and Leeds Utd were taking over at the top of English football.

Things were going so badly for Docherty's new team that, at one point, United looked almost certain to be relegated. But, the controversial Scotsman managed to ignite a

Tommy Doherty who became the fourteenth manager of Manchester United.

late rally from his Old Trafford troops that dragged them out of the relegation zone by the end of the 1972–73 season.

It proved to be only a temporary reprieve for United and, the following season, shorn of the departed Denis Law and Bobby Charlton, the Red Devils suffered the unthinkable as they were relegated from the top flight. To make matters worse, United's fate was sealed by a goal from Denis Law for his new club Manchester City in the local derby.

Docherty managed to survive the disaster of relegation and he was given the time to bring United back from the Second Division. With a number of new faces on board, he repaid the faith of the United directors by winning the Second Division at the first time of asking in 1975.

The following season, Docherty's young United side came third in the First Division and there was genuine belief that the Scot had the club back on track.

Although United could only finish sixth in the league the next year, Docherty did bring them to the FA Cup final against a much-fancied Liverpool side and with Irishmen Sammy McIlroy and Jimmy Nicholl in the side, Docherty led United to a famous 2–1 victory.

It wasn't enough to save Docherty, however, as an off-the-field affair angered the

United hierarchy and led to the former Scotland manager being sacked in the summer of 1977.

United replaced Docherty with Queens Park Rangers' manager Dave Sexton, whose four-year tenure at the club proved pretty uneventful, with the Englishman failing to lift the club back to the heights they had become used to in the 1960s.

In Sexton's first season in charge, United finished in tenth spot in the league and barely improved on that a year later by finishing ninth.

Sexton did bring United to the final of the FA Cup in 1979, when they were dramatically beaten 3–2 by Arsenal. He also came close to winning the league in 1980, when United finished runners-up to Liverpool on the final day of the season, but following an indifferent season the year after, Sexton was let go.

Off the field, United's chairman Louis Edwards died of a heart attack in 1980 and was replaced by his son, Martin, who would remain on as club chairman until 2002, by which time the club had been restored to its position as the best in England.

Gordon Hill celebrates one of his goals as United beat Derby County to make it to the 1976 FA Cup semi-final.

Dave Sexton was seen as a manager who was a safe pair of hands.

Dave Sexton's removal as manager in 1981 left United searching for another new team boss. All the club had to show in the thirteen years since being crowned European champions was a single FA Cup triumph.

Next in line for the United hot-seat was the hugely flamboyant Ron Atkinson.

Known more popularly as 'Big Ron', Atkinson had done a fantastic job with unfancied West Brom, leading them to third in the league and the quarter-finals of the UEFA Cup. His confident attitude and ability to sign big-name players for United suggested the Old Trafford hierarchy may finally have found the right man to bring success back to the club.

His first major deal in the transfer market was to snap up top Irish striker Frank Stapleton from Arsenal. Dublin-born Kevin Moran became an integral part of Atkinson's United team, whilst Paul McGrath and Norman Whiteside also played for the club during his tenure.

United finished third in the league during Atkinson's first year in charge but despite all the promise, this was as close as they would get to winning a title under Big Ron.

United showed a greater ability to succeed in the cup competitions, and they made it to the finals of both the Milk Cup and FA Cup in Atkinson's second season. His charges were beaten 2–1 by Liverpool in the Milk Cup final, but they did manage to win the FA Cup with a 4–0 replay win over Brighton.

Atkinson repeated the trick in 1985 when

The irrepressible Big Ron.

he led United to their second FA Cup win in three years by beating Everton 1–0 in the final at Wembley.

Despite these cup successes, the need for United to recapture the league crown was growing by the year and heaped more pressure on Atkinson. When United failed to make the most of a brilliant start to the 1985–86 season, Atkinson's days at Old Trafford looked to be numbered.

A poor start to the 1986–87 season sealed his fate and he was sacked as manager in November 1986.

It had been just over nineteen years since United had won the First Division title and the three FA Cup wins in that time were not enough for either United's board or fans.

Five managers had tried to pick up the baton left by Busby but, despite varying degrees of success, none had managed to bring United back to the very top in the game. As United searched for yet another new manager, all involved with the club hoped that whoever got the job next would finally lift their league title jinx.

117

Ken Doherty

66 My first really vivid memory of supporting Manchester Utd was when they beat Liverpool 2–1 in the FA Cup final in 1977. I was only eight or nine years old at the time and almost everybody in school supported either Man Utd or Liverpool.

The popularity of these two clubs in Ireland was not only because they were both very successful but also because they had a lot of Irish players. George Best was obviously the biggest name from Ireland to have played for Man Utd and, in his prime, he was the club's best ever player.

I was too young to remember Best playing in his heyday but I grew up with all the stories about him and I read the books, so he was a big hero of mine. The closest I ever got to George was when I played him in an exhibition snooker game in Dublin in 1986. He was a decent snooker player as he had played a lot of pool and it was a great thrill to meet him.

I can't exactly recall the first game I attended at Old Trafford but when I lived in London in the 1990s I used to go to a lot of games. A friend of mine knew people in Manchester and he was always able to get tickets for home games. So, I would pick him up in my car and we would make the three-hour drive up to watch the matches and then head back to London afterwards.

There were some great games during that time as United began to win the league regularly and also play some big matches in Europe.

My greatest memory from any United game was when I was lucky enough to be in Barcelona in 1999 when we won the European Cup with those two dramatic late goals against Bayern Munich.

There are other cup games that stick out as well, including an FA Cup semi-final with Oldham in 1994. Mark Hughes scored a really late equaliser to draw the game 1–1 which was a classic moment as United won the replay and then beat Chelsea in the final.

Another great game I was at was the Old Trafford clash between United and Real Madrid in 2000. Madrid were winning the tie 3-1 from the first game in Spain and had all their star players there that night including Zidane, Ronaldo, Roberto Carlos and Figo. They played extremely well at Old Trafford and were leading 3-2 in the game when David Beckham came on as a substitute

for United and scored two great goals to give us a 4-3 lead. It wasn't enough and United may have lost the tie overall, but it was still a great game to be at and the atmosphere in the ground that night was electric.

From a personal point of view, my proudest moment at Old Trafford came in 1997, when I was invited to the ground to show off the World Championship trophy I had won that year.

When I arrived at the ground, I got to meet all of the players as they were having a pre-match meal. The first man to stand up and shake my hand was the captain Eric Cantona. I was a bit taken aback by that as I didn't think he would know anything about snooker. He was also my favourite player at the time, alongside Roy Keane. Other Manchester United players that I really liked were Mark Hughes and Bryan Robson. Of the current team, my favourite two players are Paul Scholes and Ryan Giggs.

The number of Irish players at Man Utd has waned in recent years because of the increase in foreign players coming into the Premiership. That said, the foreign players who have come in have been nothing but good for the game, and they can help our guys learn how to hold on to the ball and make great passes. They have shown that football is not all about hoofing it up field to a big man up front to knock it down for a smaller guy running onto it.

But the structure in Ireland for young players is very good, so the country will continue to produce great footballers, even if they do not all end up at Man Utd.

It will be interesting to see who eventually takes over from Sir Alex Ferguson as manager as he has been such a great servant to the club. Ferguson has proven himself to be one of the best football managers of all time with everything he has achieved in the game. His life story is just so inspirational and it's no surprise to see many of his former players such as Mark Hughes, Roy Keane, Paul Ince and Steve Bruce now doing well in management. It shows that they really learned a lot from him.

It will be difficult for whoever takes over from Ferguson because no matter what they do, it will inevitably be compared with what Ferguson achieved.

Looking to the future, I would love to see Roy Keane as manager of United. He is already proving that he has what it takes to be a great manager and because he was such a brilliant player and captain of the club, it would be great to see him back there in the top role. **99**

Sammy McIlroy	
Place of birth:	Belfast
Date of birth:	2 August 1954
Position:	Forward/Midfielder
Years at United:	1971–1981
Games played:	419
Goals:	71
Hounours:	FA Cup (1977)

Exciting young Belfast forward Sammy McIlroy arrived at Manchester United at just fifteen years of age in 1969. He was brought to the club whilst only a schoolboy by Matt Busby as he continued the club's trend of bringing in the best youngsters from around the British Isles.

McIlroy's raw natural ability meant he was always destined for a big future in the game and he enjoyed almost a decade as one of United's top players.

Initially playing in a forward role, McIlroy later used his big-game intelligence to drop into a deeper midfield position where he became an important player in the United set-up.

McIlroy made his debut for United aged seventeen in November 1971, in the intense environment of the Manchester derby at Maine Road. Far from being overawed by the occasion, young McIlroy played a storming game, scoring one goal and assisting in another as United drew 3–3 with their rivals.

McIlroy's performance instantly endeared him to the United faithful and he became one of the fans' favourites throughout the 1970s.

By the end of his first season in the United team, McIlroy had played sixteen games and scored four goals as the Red Devils finished eighth in the league.

McIlroy still had to bide his time before gaining a permanent place in the United first eleven and, during his second season, the young Belfast forward was used in just ten league games without scoring as new manager Tommy Docherty was brought in to try and improve United's situation.

McIlroy played in twenty-nine league games during the ill-fated 1973–74 campaign and scored six goals but it wasn't enough to stop the club being relegated to the Second Division.

However, he was a vital member of the team that gained promotion back to the First Division in 1975 when United won the Second Division title. McIlroy played in all of United's league games during that campaign, chipping in with seven vital goals.

The next season was one of the best for McIlroy on a personal level, and he notched up ten league goals as the team finished in third place, their best position in almost a decade.

McIlroy also helped United to the FA Cup final that year by scoring against Peterborough and Wolves during the Red Devils' exciting Cup run.

Unfortunately for United, they were on the wrong end of one of the biggest FA Cup final shocks ever, when unfancied Southampton from the Second Division captured the Cup with a 1–0 win.

It was a defeat that deeply hurt United but they put it behind them to reach the final at Wembley again the following year and McIlroy played in each of United's FA Cup games, including a memorable 2–1 final win over newly crowned league champions Liverpool.

The winners' medal McIlroy received that day was his only major honour during his time with United and was easily the highlight of his Old Trafford career.

When manager Tommy Docherty left the club to be replaced by Dave Sexton, McIlroy remained a key member of the United team. He played in nearly all of United's league games under Sexton between 1977–80, scoring another twenty goals.

The closest McIlroy came to a league winners' medal was in 1980 when United finished runners-up to Liverpool. Though he did enjoy another big day out at Wembley, when United played Arsenal in the 1979 FA Cup final – a game noted for one of the best ever finishes to a cup final, and McIlroy was right in the middle of the drama.

Trailing 2–0 with five minutes to go, United pegged Arsenal back to 2–2 with McIlroy scoring a brilliant equaliser, before Alan Sunderland dramatically broke United hearts with a last-gasp winner for Arsenal.

McIlroy played on for Manchester United until February 1982, when new manager Ron Atkinson sold him to Stoke City for £350,000.

Just a few months after his move from Old Trafford, McIlroy appeared in all of Northern Ireland's games at the 1982 World Cup in Spain and he continued to play for Northern Ireland for another five years,

> **"I don't want to be anyone's assistant but I would go to Man Utd as a kit manager."**

Sammy McIlroy spells out his love of his old club when manager of Macclesfield.

becoming one of his country's best-loved servants. He also captained the team that qualified for the 1986 World Cup in Mexico.

One of Sammy McIlroy's last performances for Manchester United had been to score a hat-trick in a 5–0 demolition of Wolves at Old Trafford in March 1981. They were his last ever goals in a United shirt.

Other Clubs: Stoke, Manchester City, Orgryte IS, Bury, Preston NE, Northwich Victoria

International Record: Northern Ireland

Caps: 88

Goals: 5

Sammy McIlroy scores United's second goal in the 1979 FA Cup final by pushing the ball passed a diving Pat Jennings.

Mick Martin	
Place of birth:	Dublin
Date of birth:	9 July 1951
Position:	Midfield/Defender
Years at United:	1973–1975
Games played:	43
Goals:	2

Midfielder Mick Martin arrived at Manchester United in 1973, as the club was desperately trying to maintain its status in the First Division.

Signed by Tommy Docherty for £25,000 from Bohemians, Martin went straight into a United team that was staring relegation in the face. He remained a constant presence in the side that year, as United turned their season around with an amazing run of wins to avoid the drop.

Martin came from excellent footballing stock – his father Con had also been an Irish international footballer during the 1940s and 1950s – and he made his United debut in a 0–0 draw against Everton in January 1973 and helped himself to two crucial goals during that season.

Martin scored in a 2–1 home win over Newcastle Utd and repeated the trick as Man Utd beat Norwich City 1–0 at Old Trafford in early April. The win over Norwich proved particularly crucial, as they were involved in the desperate relegation battle with United.

The six points garnered from Martin's two goals went a long way to keeping his new club in the top flight, and United eventually finished fifth from the bottom, ahead of Norwich who were relegated.

A versatile player, Martin could play either in midfield or anywhere in defence when called upon, but found his first-team chances limited during his second season with the Red Devils. It was a season that won't go down as one of United's most memorable, as they suffered the unthinkable horror of relegation.

After initially losing his place in the team, Martin returned to the side during the latter stages of that campaign to help United to wins over Sheffield Utd, Chelsea and Everton. It was too little too late, however, as United began the 1974–75 season in the Second Division.

Martin's presence in the side during its season in the Second Division was sporadic, as manager Tommy Docherty brought in a number of new faces. Martin helped United get off to a great start with wins over Millwall, Portsmouth and Cardiff, but found himself out of the team for lengthy spells after this and made just nine appearances in total for United that season.

His last game for United came in a 3–2 win over Oldham in March 1975.

At the start of the following season, Martin was loaned out to John Giles' West Brom, and the deal was made permanent in December 1975.

Other Clubs: Home Farm, West Brom, Newcastle
International Record: Republic of Ireland
Caps: 52
Goals: 4

Jimmy Nicholl	
Place of birth:	Ontario, Canada
Date of birth:	28 February 1956
Position:	Right full-back
Years at United:	1971–1981
Games played:	248
Goals:	6
Honours:	FA Cup (1977)

Canadian-born Northern Ireland international Jimmy Nicholl arrived at Manchester United as a youth player in 1971.

A talented right-back, Nicholl could also play as a centre-half when needed, and he etched out a great career for himself at Old Trafford, winning an FA Cup winners' medal along the way.

Nicholl made his debut for United at the age of just nineteen when the Red Devils beat Southampton 1–0 in a league game in April 1975.

Starting as a substitute at the beginning of the 1975–76 season, it didn't take Nicholl long to make the right-back berth his own at United as he became an important member of the team.

He also made his debut for Northern Ireland against Israel in March 1976 and became a stalwart in the team for the following ten

Jimmy Nicholl pats Liam Brady on the back during the 1979 FA Cup final.

years, which proved to be some of the best years in Northern Irish football. Nicholl played in every game his country played in both the 1982 and 1986 World Cup finals.

In the meantime, Nicholl helped United to the final of the 1976 FA Cup with wins over Oxford Utd and Wolves, but he did not feature at Wembley when United were humbled 1–0 by Southampton.

Nicholl remained United's first-choice right-back as they returned to Wembley a year later to play Liverpool in the FA Cup final. He did a great job in shackling Liverpool's

feared attack as United ran out 2–1 winners.

The following season, Nicholl played in thirty-nine of United's forty-two league games and even pitched in with a goal in the Manchester derby, despite United losing the game 3–1.

Nicholl scored again against Aston Villa and helped himself to another rare goal against Porto in an impressive 5–2 European Cup Winners' Cup win for United at Old Trafford.

The goals dried up for Nicholl over the next two seasons, although he remained an important member of the team. He was a

Jimmy Nicholl and Tommy Cavanagh celebrate winning the 1977 FA Cup with Tommy Docherty

permanent fixture as Dave Sexton's United ran Liverpool close for the league title in 1980, eventually having to settle for second place.

Sexton was let go by United a year later and Nicholl's time at the club was over soon after. New boss Ron Atkinson sold him to Canadian club Toronto Blizzard for £250,000 in April 1982.

Other Clubs: Sunderland, Toronto Blizzard, Rangers, West Brom, Dunfermline, Raith Rovers

International Record: Northern Ireland

Caps: 73

Goals: 1

David McCreery	
Place of birth:	Belfast
Date of birth:	16 September 1957
Position:	Midfielder
Years at United:	1972–1978
Games played:	110
Goals:	8
Honours:	FA Cup (1977)

When David McCreery signed as a schoolboy for Manchester United in 1972, he was following a long tradition of Belfast youngsters to sign up for the club as apprentices.

The fifteen-year-old midfielder moved to Old Trafford at a time when George Best was still the main attraction and fellow Belfast boy Sammy McIlroy was breaking into the team as a teenage sensation.

Like McIlroy, McCreery would make his United debut when still only seventeen years old, when he came on a second-half substitute in a 0–0 with Portsmouth in November 1974. United had just been relegated to the Second Division and manager Tommy Docherty

was keen to use a settled side in a bid to win promotion.

Because of this, young McCreery only starred in one more game for United that season – a 3–0 win over Blackpool – as he continued his learning curve in the reserve team.

When United won promotion to the First Division, McCreery was himself promoted into the first team, where he became a regular alongside McIlroy, Gerry Daly and Lou Macari.

McCreery's first goal for United couldn't have come at a better time. He scored in a 2–2 derby draw with Man City at Maine Road in September 1975.

McCreery showed he had a good scoring touch when he found the net again later in the season in a 4–0 win for United over West Ham and notched up another two in impressive wins over Middlesbrough and Everton respectively.

McCreery had also played his part in helping United reach the FA Cup final in 1976 with wins over Leicester City followed by Derby County in the semi-final. In the final against Southampton, McCreery started on the bench and came on for Gordon Hill

Dave McCreery.

in the second half as United were beaten by a late Bobby Stokes goal.

McCreery was in and out of the side at the start of the 1976–77 season, although he did manage to score again at Maine Road as United recorded a famous 3–1 derby win.

He scored just once more for United that season in a 3–3 draw with Stoke, as the Red Devils finished a disappointing sixth.

The club had managed to make it back to Wembley for the FA Cup final and, like the previous year, McCreery started the game as a substitute. Amazingly, he again came on a second-half sub for Gordon Hill but this time his United side tasted glory by beating Liverpool 2–1.

Tommy Docherty's sudden departure after the Cup final win meant McCreery started the following season under new boss Dave Sexton.

For the third time in a row, McCreery was a substitute as United played at Wembley, this time in a 0–0 draw with Liverpool in the Charity Shield. As in previous years, McCreery's opportunities in the United midfield were limited and he played in just fifteen league games that season under Sexton, scoring just one goal.

However, he had become an important part of the Northern Ireland midfield by the late 1970s and enjoyed successive World Cup qualifications in 1982 and 1986.

David McCreery remained at Manchester United until the end of the 1978–79 season, during which he had played in fifteen games, without scoring any goals. His last game for United came in a 1–1 draw with Chelsea at Old Trafford in May 1979.

Three months later, McCreery was sold to Queens Park Rangers for £200,000, having played 110 games for United, scoring eight goals.

Other Clubs: Queens Park Rangers, Tulsa Roughnecks, Newcastle Utd, Hearts, Hartlepool
International Record: Northern Ireland
Caps: 67
Goals: 0

Gerry Daly	
Place of birth:	Dublin
Date of birth:	30 April 1954
Position:	Midfield/Forward
Years at United:	1973–1977
Games played:	142
Goals:	32

Attacking midfielder Gerry Daly made the move from Bohemians to Manchester Utd for £20,000 in 1973. Though, unfortunately, his arrival coincided with a time when the club was in turmoil as they battled relegation.

As a midfielder with an eye for goal, Daly became an integral part of the United revival in the mid-1970s, which culminated in the team reaching two FA Cup finals on the trot. But first Daly had to suffer the pain of relegation before things began to get better.

Gerry Daly beats the Derby County defence in the 1976 FA Cup semi-final.

By the time Daly made his debut in August 1973, star player George Best was almost on his way out, as United's European Cup-winning team of five years previously fell apart. That first game came in a 3–0 defeat to Arsenal, as the Red Devils struggled under manager Tommy Docherty.

In fact, Daly was on the losing side in his first four matches with United that season and the team only picked up two wins in his first ten games there.

Daly's first goal for United arrived in a crucial 3–1 league win over Chelsea in March 1974. After which, he helped United to another

three wins in the league the following month but it was all too late and the Red Devils paid for their poor start by being relegated.

In his second season at Old Trafford, Daly became a vital member of a team aiming for instant promotion back to the First Division and United started the season on fire, thanks to his scoring exploits. He notched up a hat-trick in a 4–0 home win over Millwall in August 1974 and also scored the winning goals in United's next two games against Portsmouth and Cardiff as the Red Devils roared to the top of the table.

A month later, Daly had scored the winner

against Millwall again and added to this with the only goal in a 1–0 League Cup win over local rivals Manchester City. United enjoyed a decent run in the League Cup that year with Daly in the side as they made it as far as the semi-final, before bowing out to Norwich City.

More importantly, however, United maintained their form in the league and won the Second Division with Daly having played in thirty-seven games during the season, scoring eleven goals.

Daly's most impressive season at United came a year later, when he helped Tommy Docherty's men finish third in the league and reach the FA Cup final against Southampton.

He scored two goals in a 3–2 win over Tottenham at Old Trafford in September 1975, as United returned to the First Division with a flourish. But his most important goals that year came in the FA Cup. He scored both United's goals in a third-round 2–1 victory over Oxford Utd and was also on the scoresheet as United overcame Leicester City 2–1 in the fifth round.

Daly's impressive scoring form continued as he notched up another FA Cup goal in a drawn quarter-final with Wolves. He then helped United to win the replay 3–2 and was also in the side when they beat Derby County 2–0 in the semi-final to reach Wembley.

United were firm favourites going into the final with Southampton, but Daly was to end up disappointed as his side lost the game 1–0.

He remained part of the United side at the start of the 1976–77 season – scoring four goals in seventeen league games – before Tommy Docherty made the decision to sell him to Derby County in March 1977.

Ironically, his last game for United had been in a 3–1 win over Derby a month earlier.

During his time at United, Daly notched up a total of thirty-two goals – an excellent strike rate for a midfielder.

Other Clubs: Stella Marris, Bohemians, Derby County, Shrewsbury, Doncaster Utd
International Record: Republic of Ireland
Caps: 48
Goals: 13

Trevor Anderson	
Place of birth:	Belfast
Date of birth:	3 March 1951
Position:	Forward
Years at United:	1972–1974
Games played:	19
Goals:	2

Forward Trevor Anderson was brought to Manchester United in a £20,000 deal in October 1972 after impressing with his play for the Irish League side Portadown.

He arrived just a couple of months before United boss Frank O'Farrell was sacked and replaced by charismatic Scot Tommy Docherty. Anderson's opportunities under the new manager were limited as Docherty chose to use the more experienced forward players he had at his disposal.

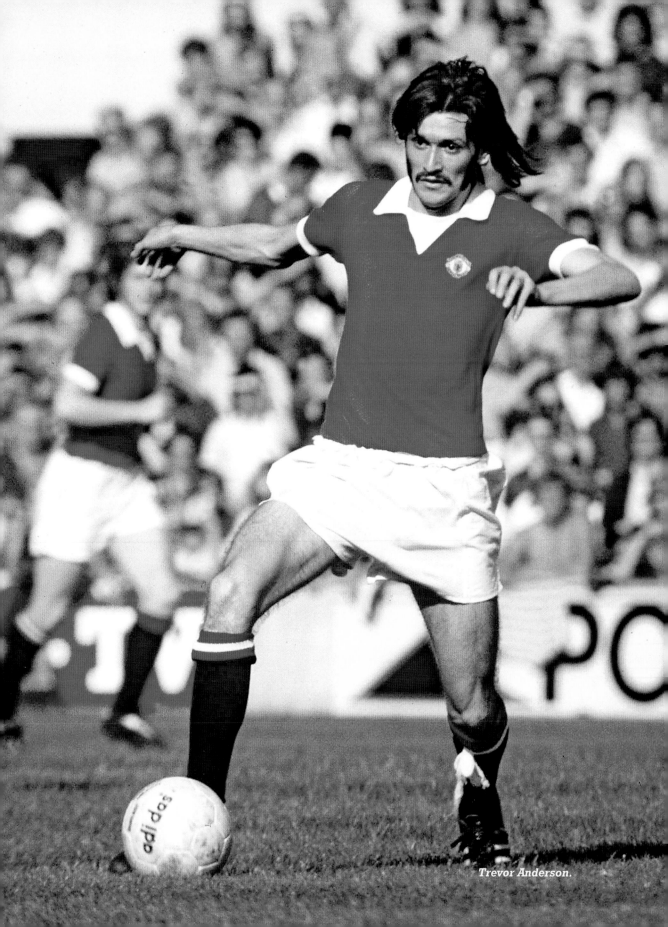

Trevor Anderson.

However, the young striker finally made his debut for United in a 2–0 win over Southampton in March 1973 and he kept his place in the team as United remained unbeaten in the first six games he was involved in – a mini revival which managed to stave off relegation from the First Division that year.

Anderson's first goal for United was extremely crucial, as it proved to be the winner in a 1–0 win over Leeds Utd that went a long way to helping the club's survival mission that year.

The following season, Anderson was initially involved in the team, playing in twelve of United's league games before Christmas 1973, scoring just the one goal in a 2–1 defeat to Ipswich. But, by the turn of the year, he was out of manager Tommy Docherty's plans and didn't play at all as United slumped into the Second Division.

Anderson's last game for United came in a 0–0 draw with Southampton at Old Trafford on 8 December 1973. He remained at United for the beginning of the 1974–75 season before being sold to Swindon Town in November 1974.

Other Clubs: Portadown, Swindon Town, Peterborough, Linfield
International Record: Northern Ireland
Caps: 22
Goals: 4

Paddy Roche	
Place of birth:	Dublin
Date of birth:	4 January 1951
Position:	Goalkeeper
Years at United:	1973–1982
Games played:	56
Goals:	0
Honours:	FA Cup (1977)

Dublin-born goalkeeper Paddy Roche was signed by Manchester United from Shelbourne in October 1973 for £15,000.

It took new boss Tommy Docherty over two years to give Roche his chance in the United goal, as he preferred to use the experienced Alex Stepney, but Roche eventually made his debut under Docherty in a Second Division game against Oxford in August 1975, which United lost 1–0.

Roche got his first taste of Old Trafford action a week later, when he kept a clean sheet in a 2–0 win for the Red Devils over Hull City. These were the only two games that Roche played for United that season as the club won promotion back into the top flight by winning the Second Division.

Roche reappeared in the United goal for a brief period in November 1976 when he played in five games in succession.

Unfortunately, things didn't go so well for him during this period, as United were beaten 3–1 by arch rivals Liverpool at Anfield and, worse still, 4–0 by Man City in a League Cup game at Maine Road.

Roche remained at Old Trafford as under-

study to Stepney as United made it to two FA Cup finals in a row, in 1976 and 1977. Roche didn't play a part in either final but did manage to get more game time following the departure of Tommy Docherty in the summer of 1977.

Under new boss Dave Sexton, Roche played in nineteen of United's league games in the 1978–79 season, keeping four clean sheets. However, Alex Stepney remained Sexton's first choice keeper when fit, limiting

Roche to just sixteen games the following season.

Nevertheless, Roche remained at United and played two more games under Sexton as they ran Liverpool close for the league title in 1980.

Roche was still at United when new manager Ron Atkinson came in 1981 but his time at the club was beginning to wind down. He played just three games for Atkinson before being let go to Brentford in August 1982.

Roche's last game for United finished in a 3–2 defeat to Southampton in December 1981.

During his nine years at the club, Roche played in goal for United a total of fifty-six times and kept eleven clean sheets.

Other Clubs: Shelbourne, Brentford
International Record: Republic of Ireland
Caps: 8
Goals: 0

Tommy Jackson	
Place of birth:	Antrim
Date of birth:	3 November 1946
Position:	Midfield
Years at United:	1975–1978
Games played:	23
Goals:	0

Northern Ireland midfielder Tommy Jackson arrived at United after a successful playing career with Everton and Nottingham Forest.

Manchester United had just been promoted back into the First Division and manager Tommy Docherty brought twenty-nine-year-old Jackson in to add steel and experience to his midfield.

Despite their brief sojourn into the depths of the Second Division, expectations at United were still high but Jackson was not fazed, having already won a league title and played in the European Cup for Everton.

He made his debut for United in August 1975, helping his new team to a 2–0 win over Wolves. He made an equally successful debut at Old Trafford with a 5–1 win over Sheffield

Utd as Man Utd made an excellent start to the new season, remaining unbeaten in the first seven games that Jackson was involved in.

The team continued their good form in the League Cup as they knocked out Brentford and Aston Villa with Jackson in the side. However, things took a turn for the worse for Jackson when he was in the United side hammered 4–0 by Manchester City in the League Cup in November 1975.

Jackson spent some time out of the team after this and didn't appear again until April 1976, when United beat Burnley 1–0 in a league game. A month later, Jackson was in the United side that buried the ghost of the awful League Cup defeat to Man City as United enjoyed a 2–0 derby day win over their rivals at Old Trafford.

In all, Jackson appeared in seventeen league games for United that season as they finished third in the First Division.

United also made it to the final of the FA Cup in 1976 but Jackson did not play any part in the campaign, as the Red Devils were beaten by Southampton in the final.

Jackson's appearances in the United team the following season were limited. He only played his first game in a 3–0 League Cup defeat to Everton in December 1976 and didn't appear again until near the end of that campaign when he came into the United midfield for a 1–1 draw with Burnley.

On 11 May 1977, Jackson played his last game for United in a 3–3 draw away to Stoke City. He remained at the club for another year, before being allowed a free transfer to Waterford in the League of Ireland in June 1978.

Other Clubs: Everton, Notts Forest, Waterford Utd
International Record: Northern Ireland
Caps: 35
Goals: 0

Chris McGrath	
Place of birth:	Belfast
Date of birth:	29 November 1954
Position:	Winger
Years at United:	1976–1981
Games played:	34
Goals:	1

Chris McGrath arrived at Manchester United in October 1976 after spending three years as a flying winger with Tottenham. Already a senior Northern Ireland international, United manager Tommy Docherty splashed out £30,000 to bring McGrath to Old Trafford to add to the team's attacking options.

McGrath made his debut in the same month he signed for United, when he came on as a substitute in a 2–2 draw at home to Norwich City on 23 October. Four days later, he again came off the bench as United rammed in seven goals in an emphatic 7–2 League Cup win over Newcastle United.

His first start for United came in a 3–2

defeat in the league away to Aston Villa in November 1976, but Docherty mostly used McGrath as an impact sub from the bench. He appeared in just eight games in total for United in the 1976–77 season and did not feature at all in the FA Cup campaign that United won with victory over Liverpool.

When Docherty left United that summer, McGrath returned for the following season under new manager Dave Sexton but still could not nail down a permanent place in the team. That said, McGrath did have his best run in the United side that year as he helped them to some memorable wins at Old Trafford.

McGrath had helped United to beat top French club St Etienne 2–0 in the Cup Winners' Cup and was also back in the side when United faced Porto at Old Trafford in October 1977. Unfortunately, United had a massive mountain to climb that night, after losing 4–0 in the first leg in Portugal, but McGrath and his team-mates came agonisingly close to pulling off a miraculous escape with a 5–2 victory at Old Trafford.

It was a rare bit of excitement for United at the time as they failed to ignite in the league under Sexton.

McGrath appeared in sixteen league games during the 1977–78 season, as the team finished well off the pace in tenth place. One of those appearances led to his only goal for the club in a 2–1 defeat to West Ham in December 1977.

Chris McGrath remained at United until

1981, but only played a handful more games in the first team. After he played in a couple of games at the start of the 1978–79 season he disappeared for almost two years, before reappearing in the United side.

His last appearance for United came in a 0–0 draw with Birmingham in August 1980. A few months later, McGrath's contract at United was terminated and he signed up to play for Tulsa Roughnecks in the USA in February 1981.

Other Clubs: Tottenham, Tulsa Roughnecks
International Record: Northern Ireland
Caps: 21
Goals: 4

Thomas Connell	
Place of birth:	Newry
Date of birth:	25 November 1957
Position:	Full-back
Years at United:	1978–1982
Games played:	2
Goals:	0

Tough-tackling left-back Thomas Connell joined Manchester United from Irish League side Coleraine in August 1978 and was one of five players United manager Dave Sexton brought to the club that summer, including fellow Ulstermen Tom Sloan and the teenager Norman Whiteside.

Connell, normally a left-back, could also play as a central defender if needed and Sexton used him in the first-team squad during his first year at Old Trafford.

Connell made two appearances for United during the 1978–79 season, but was on the losing side on both occasions. He made his debut away to Bolton on 22 December 1978 but United were on the wrong end of a 3–0 defeat. Connell kept his place in the team for United's St Stephen's (Boxing) Day clash with Liverpool at Old Trafford four days later, but again United lost the game 3–0.

At the turn of the year, Connell was back in the United reserve team, playing in the Central League and made no more appearances for the first team that season when they finished ninth in the First Division.

Connell remained in the United reserves for the rest of Sexton's tenure as manager and he struggled to gain a permanent place in the first team.

When Sexton was replaced by Ron Atkinson, Connell's chances were reduced even further. The new manager placed him on the transfer list and, in July 1982, Irish League side Glentoran paid £37,000 to bring Connell back home.

Other Clubs: Coleraine, Glentoran, Portadown
International Record: Northern Ireland
Caps: 1
Goals: 0

Ashley Grimes	
Place of birth:	Dublin
Date of birth:	2 August 1957
Position:	Left full-back
Years at United:	1977–1983
Games played:	107
Goals:	11
Honours:	FA Cup (1983)

Left-back Ashley Grimes' career at Manchester United proves there is truth in the saying that if first you don't succeed, try, try, and try again.

A tough-tackling and energetic full-back, who could also play on the left of midfield, Grimes first arrived at Old Trafford as a fifteen-year-old schoolboy in 1972 desperate for a chance at the big time with Manchester United. Unfortunately for young Grimes, it didn't work out at the time and he moved home to Dublin, where he continued to play for Bohemians.

Five years after that initial contact, Grimes continued to impress for Bohs and United boss Tommy Docherty was eventually convinced to bring him back to Manchester in a £20,000 deal in 1977. It was an extremely exciting move for Grimes, as United had just being crowned FA Cup winners with victory over Liverpool at Wembley. However, Docherty soon made a shock departure from United and was replaced by former Queens Park Rangers boss Dave Sexton.

Grimes made his debut for United on August 1977 away to Birmingham, when he

came off the bench to help his team wrap up a comfortable 4–1 win.

As with many of the other young Irish players who had arrived in England, Grimes was given time to settle in at Old Trafford. He played in thirteen league games for the club in his first season, scoring two goals, as the Red Devils finished way off the pace in tenth place behind league winners Nottingham Forest.

Things didn't get too much better for United the following season, when they again finished in mid-table obscurity. Grimes played in sixteen games that season as United finished in ninth place.

Grimes' best season with United came in 1979–80, when the club came within a whisker of taking the league title from Liverpool, finishing just two points behind in second place. Grimes played in twenty-six of United's forty-two league games that season, chipping in with another three goals as Dave Sexton's side put in a determined challenge for the title.

When United could only finish eighth the following season, with Grimes only fleetingly involved, Sexton was replaced by the flamboyant Ron Atkinson and things began to look up for the Red Devils.

Atkinson immediately brought in some top names such as Bryan Robson and United finished third in the league in his first season in charge, with Grimes playing in eleven league matches.

Grimes' final season at United was probably the most eventful.

The Red Devils failed to make any inroads

Ashley Grimes.

on winning a league title but they did make it to Wembley for two cup finals in 1983. The Milk Cup final tussle with arch rivals Liverpool starred five Irishmen – Kevin Moran, Frank Stapleton, Norman Whiteside, Mark Lawrenson and Ronnie Whelan – but Grimes failed to make it into the United squad which lost the game 2–1.

When United returned to Wembley in May 1983 to take on Brighton in the FA Cup final, Grimes was an unused sub. The game finished 2–2 and Grimes was again an unused sub as United won the replay 4–0.

At the end of the 1982–83 season, Grimes was sold to Coventry City for a fee of £200,000.

During his 107 games for Manchester United, Ashley Grimes had managed to score eleven goals and won one FA Cup winners' medal.

Other Clubs: Bohemians, Coventry City, Luton Town, Osasuna
International Record: Republic of Ireland
Caps: 18
Goals: 1

Tom Sloan	
Place of birth:	Ballymena
Date of birth:	10 July 1959
Position:	Midfielder
Years at United:	1978–1983
Games played:	12
Goals:	0

Pacey midfielder Tom Sloan moved to Manchester United in August 1978 in a £20,000 deal from Ballymena. He was highly regarded in the Irish League, having burst onto the scene as a teenager playing for Ballymena Utd, and Man Utd just pipped Spurs to his signature.

Even though Sloan was only nineteen when he arrived at Old Trafford, he made his debut early when he deputised for the injured Lou Macari. United manager Dave Sexton threw Sloan into the side for a league game against Ipswich at Old Trafford in November 1978, which the Red Devils won 2–0.

Sloan impressed on his debut and remained in the United side for a clash with Everton at Goodison Park three days later that ended in a 3–0 defeat. He appeared in just one more game for United in 1978, when he came on as a second-half substitute for Jimmy Greenhoff in a 5–3 defeat to West Brom at Old Trafford on 30 December.

His next start for United was in a 1–1 draw with Southampton in April 1979, but, after this, Sloan was mainly used from the substitutes' bench.

Things remained the same at the beginning of the 1979–80 season when Sloan came off the bench to help United to impressive 4–0 and 2–0 home wins over Stoke City and Bolton respectively.

Sloan made a rare appearance in United's first eleven for an away game against Ipswich which United lost 6–0.

Tom Sloan.

Kevin Moran.

United faired extremely well in the league that year, however, just missing out on the title to Liverpool on the last day of the season. But throughout the season Sloan was only a bit-part player and made only five appearances in the league.

Sloan's situation never really improved and he made just three appearances in the 1980–81 season, one of which was a 1–0 League Cup defeat to Coventry.

His last game for United came in a 0–0 home draw with Coventry on 8 November 1980.

Sloan remained at United for another year under new boss Ron Atkinson but did not play in any games and Atkinson eventually allowed Sloan to leave for Fourth Division side Chester City in December 1982.

Other Clubs: Chester City
International Record: Northern Ireland
Caps: 3
Goals: 0

Kevin Moran	
Place of birth:	Dublin
Date of birth:	29 April 1956
Position:	Central defender
Years at United:	1978–1988
Games played:	289
Goals:	24
Honours:	FA Cup (1983, 1985)

Few young Irishmen could have been better prepared for the red-hot atmosphere of Old Trafford than defender Kevin Moran.

He arrived over at Manchester in 1978 at the age of twenty-two, but had already had a few years of big-game experience through playing Gaelic Football for his native county. The multi-talented Moran was part of the renowned Dublin side which enjoyed some mammoth Croke Park encounters with Kerry during the late 1970s. By the time he arrived at Old Trafford, Moran already had two All-Ireland winning medals tucked away in his back pocket.

Moran had been spotted by Man Utd's Irish scout Billy Behan, who convinced manager Dave Sexton to sign him in 1978.

It took Moran over a year to adjust to his new surroundings but he eventually made his debut against Southampton in a league game in April 1979.

A month later, Man Utd lost 3–2 to Arsenal in one of the most memorable finishes to an FA Cup final, but Moran was not involved.

He continued to struggle to break into the United team during the 1979–80 season, making only a brief flurry of appearances at the centre of defence. However, he did manage to score his first goal for the club at this time, during a 5–0 drubbing of Norwich City at Old Trafford.

Moran was back out of the side at the beginning of 1980, but returned to first-team action for three games at the end of April, deputising for tough Scot Gordon McQueen. He also helped United to three victories to secure runners-up spot behind Liverpool in the league.

Moran eventually broke into the United team in the 1980–81 season, when he started thirty-two of the club's forty-two league games. But, by the end of the season, manager Dave Sexton had been sacked as United struggled to make any real impact in the league, or do well in the cup competitions.

Moran was initially left out of the team by Sexton's replacement Ron Atkinson, but the new manager soon realised Moran's excellent qualities in defence and he became a fixture in 'Big Ron's' new-look team.

Whilst mostly admired for his stout defending, Moran also had the happy knack of scoring the odd goal, as he did in a memorable 2–1 league victory over Liverpool in 1982.

The following season, Moran was a com-

manding figure in the heart of a United defence that brought the team to both the Milk Cup and FA Cup finals at Wembley.

Moran was to endure cup final heartache against Liverpool in the Milk Cup, when United lost 2–1 in extra time, but more than made up for it with a 4–0 victory over Brighton in the FA Cup final replay.

With the FA Cup win firmly behind them, Moran's United started the 1983–84 full of hope that they could finally win the club's first league title in almost two decades. United did put in a strong challenge, winning twenty of their forty-two league games and losing only eight, but could still only manage a fourth-place finish, six points behind winners Liverpool.

Moran was part of the United side that made it to the semi-finals of the European

Referee Peter Willis is surrounded by players from both Everton and Manchester Utd as he sends off Kevin Moran in the 1985 FA Cup final.

Cup Winners' Cup in 1984, before bowing out to Italian giants Juventus.

Fourth place was again the best United could finish in the league the following year, but Moran was part of the United team that played in their second FA Cup final in three years.

The final was an eagerly anticipated contest with newly crowned league champions Everton, but it is one which Moran will remember for all the wrong reasons.

He had the misfortune of becoming the first player ever to be sent off in an FA Cup final, for a clumsy late challenge on Everton midfielder Peter Reid.

Luckily, Moran's red card didn't stop United going on to win the game 1–0 through a brilliant goal from Norman Whiteside. But it did preclude him from receiving a winners' medal on the day, though he was eventually presented with one from the club.

United began the 1985–86 season in good form, but Moran often found himself out of the team through injury. United had made a blistering start to their league campaign, but by the time Moran was fit again, they had fallen away and could again only finish in fourth place.

Manager Ron Atkinson was subsequently replaced by fiery Scot Alex Ferguson – Moran's third manager during his United career.

> "People always remember you for certain things and if you're the first to do something like getting sent off in an FA Cup final, naturally you're going to be remembered more for that than anything else."

Kevin Moran, on why he's never let forget that infamous red card in the 1985 FA Cup final.

Ferguson initially took a shine to Moran, playing him for much of his first year in charge, but United finished way off the pace back in eleventh spot.

Moran was eventually allowed to leave Old Trafford on a free transfer to Sporting Gijon in Spain in 1988.

While his time at United may have been drawing to a close, Moran enjoyed a fabulous career with the Republic of Ireland, playing in both the Euro '88 and World Cup 1990 campaigns.

Together with Mick McCarthy, Moran formed part of a tough central defensive partnership that snuffed out England in the famous 1–0 win for Ireland at Euro '88. But perhaps his biggest game for Ireland came in a 1–0 defeat to Italy in Rome in the quarter-finals of the World Cup in 1990.

He was also a member of the Irish squad that made the last sixteen in the World Cup in 1994.

Kevin Moran made his final appearance for Manchester United in a 1–0 defeat at Norwich City on 5 March 1988.

Other Clubs: Sporting Gijon, Blackburn Rovers
International Record: Republic of Ireland
Caps: 71
Goals: 6

Norman Whiteside	
Place of birth:	Belfast
Date of birth:	7 May 1965
Position:	Midfield/Forward
Years at United:	1978–1989
Games played:	274
Goals:	67
Honours:	FA Cup (1983, 1985)

Norman Whiteside was brought to Manchester United as a schoolboy in September 1978 and went on to become one of the most popular figures at Old Trafford throughout the 1980s. Blessed with a powerful shot, quick mind, heading ability and tremendous strength, Whiteside made his United debut while still only sixteen years old.

Manager Ron Atkinson threw him in at the deep end and Whiteside responded with some excellent performances for the club.

His debut came against Brighton & Hove Albion in April 1982 and he followed this up with his first goal for the club in a 2–0 win over Stoke City a fortnight later.

His performances even earned Whiteside a place in the Northern Ireland team that played at the 1982 World Cup in Spain. He made his international debut against Yugoslavia at this World Cup, and became the youngest player to star in the finals at the time. Whiteside played in all of Northern Ireland's games at the tournament, including their memorable 1–0 win over hosts Spain.

When he returned from the World Cup, Whiteside kept his place in the United team as the new season came around. His versatility and strength meant he could play either on the wing, in midfield or as a supporting striker and he had a great eye for goal.

He started the 1982–83 season with four goals in his first five games, including two in a 3–1 home win over Ipswich which endeared him to the United fans.

United were proving to be a tough nut to crack in cup competitions under Ron Atkinson and Whiteside helped them advance to the latter stages of the Milk Cup and FA Cup in 1983.

He scored a goal against Arsenal in the semi-final of the Milk Cup as United won 6–3 on aggregate, and scored an equally vital goal in a 1–0 win for United against Derby County in the fifth round of the FA Cup. He then scored a brilliant winner against Arsenal in the semi-final of the competition as United advanced to the final with a 2–1 win.

His remarkable ability to score in the big games continued, as he notched up another against Liverpool in the final of the Milk Cup,

> "The only thing I have in common with George Best is that we come from the same place, play for the same club, and were discovered by the same man."

Norman Whiteside, bemoaning the dreaded 'New George Best' tag.

Norman Whiteside makes his debut for United against Brighton & Hove Albion, at the age of sixteen.

which United lost 2–1. However, Whiteside was back at Wembley as United drew 2–2 with Brighton in the FA Cup final and, true to form, he scored in the replay, which was also played at Wembley, as United won 4–0.

Whiteside had played in fifty-seven of United's sixty games that season and scored an impressive fifteen goals.

He returned to Wembley in August 1983 as United got their season off to the perfect start with a 2–0 Charity Shield victory over Liverpool, thanks to two goals from Bryan Robson. The highlight for Whiteside that season was scoring in the semi-final of the European Cup Winners' Cup against Italian

side Juventus. Unfortunately, United lost the tie 3–2 on aggregate.

Whiteside remained one of the team's best players as they set off on another FA Cup run in 1985. He scored a magnificent hat-trick as United overcame West Ham 4–2 in the quarter-final of the FA Cup, but saved his best form for the final against Everton.

In a game that was locked at 0–0 in extra time, Whiteside scored one of the most memorable goals ever in a FA Cup final. With a breakthrough in the game looking unlikely, Whiteside picked the ball up on the right side of the field. Using his tremendous strength, he advanced to the corner of the Everton

Whiteside holds aloft the 1985 FA Cup. His goal scored in extra time is one of the best scored in at Wembley.

penalty area and unleashed a sweet, curling left-foot shot into the far corner of Neville Southall's goal.

It proved to be the only goal of the game and it earned Whiteside the Goal of the Season award.

It also proved to be the major highlight of his career.

After United failed to live up to their promise under Ron Atkinson, new manager Alex Ferguson was brought into the club in November 1986.

Whiteside featured quite heavily under Ferguson's initial stewardship and captained

the side in Bryan Robson's absence as they finished second in the league in his first full year in charge. However, a recurrent knee problem kept Whiteside out of the team for over a year from March 1987. He made his return in April 1989 in a 1–1 draw with Arsenal, but Ferguson was already beginning to make changes to the team.

Whiteside no longer featured in Ferguson's plans and he was sold to Everton for £600,000 in August 1989.

During his eight years playing at United, Whiteside had proved himself one of the club's best players. Not only had he become

the youngest man to play for the club, he was also United's youngest ever scorer in both the League and FA cup finals.

His stunning goal against Everton in the 1985 FA Cup final has also ensured him a prime place in United's illustrious history.

Other Clubs: Everton
International Record: Northern Ireland
Caps: 38
Goals: 9

Tony Whelan	
Place of birth:	Dublin
Date of birth:	23 November 1959
Position:	Defender
Years at United:	1980–1983
Games played:	1
Goals:	0

Dublin-born defender Tony Whelan arrived at Manchester United in August 1980 as boss Dave Sexton attempted to beef up his defensive options.

Whelan had spent a year playing in the League of Ireland with Bohemians and had done enough in that time to catch the eye of Sexton, who paid £30,000 to bring him to Old Trafford.

Despite being one of the top defenders in Ireland at the time, Whelan was always going to find it difficult to break into a United defence that already included Kevin Moran, Gordon McQueen and Martin Buchan.

United had finished second in the league under Sexton the season before and, in spite of the manager's defensive style, there was genuine hope that Whelan's new team could go one step further.

He spent much of his first season at United on the periphery of the team, often making it onto the substitutes' bench. He did manage to play one game that year, when he came on as a sub in a 1–1 draw with Southampton at Old Trafford in November 1980.

Unfortunately for Whelan, it was the only time he would experience first-team action during his time at United.

After a poor start to their league campaign in 1981, United's manager Dave Sexton was let go and replaced by Ron Atkinson, who had his own ideas about who he wanted in his defence. Unfortunately for Whelan, he didn't feature in those plans.

When his fellow Dub Paul McGrath was brought into the United set-up in 1982, Whelan's chances grew even slimmer. He remained at United until the end of the 1982–83 season, after which he was transferred to Shamrock Rovers in the League of Ireland in June 1983.

Other Clubs: Bohemians, Shamrock Rovers, Shelbourne, Bray Wanderers

Top Ten Green Devils Goalscorers

George Best – 179	Roy Keane – 51
Frank Stapleton – 78	Denis Irwin – 33
Sammy McIlroy – 71	Gerry Daly – 32
Norman Whiteside – 67	Jackie Blanchflower – 27
Liam Whelan – 52	Kevin Moran – 24

Frank Stapleton	
Place of birth:	Dublin
Date of birth:	10 July 1956
Position:	Striker
Years at United:	1981–1987
Games played:	288
Goals:	78
Honours:	FA Cup (1983, 1985)

Striker Frank Stapleton joined Manchester United in 1981 after an illustrious six-year career at top London club Arsenal. Ironically, he had joined Arsenal as a young apprentice in 1972 after being turned down by Manchester United and, when he arrived at Old Trafford nine years later, the club had to shell out £900,000 for his services.

During his time at Arsenal, Stapleton had also scored one of the London clubs goals in a famous 3–2 FA Cup final win over United in 1979. Despite this, Stapleton set about winning over the hearts of the United fans with his busy all-action style and powerful heading technique.

The Dubliner was Ron Atkinson's first big signing for United and Stapleton would go on to help the club win two FA cups in the following four years.

Far from being a prolific striker for United, Stapleton never managed more than fourteen league goals in any one season that he was at the club. Nevertheless, his selfless running and great awareness ensured he was always appreciated.

153

Stapleton scored his first goal for United in a 2–1 home defeat to Ipswich, as the club made a sluggish start to the 1981–82 season. The team picked up the pace after this defeat, however, and Stapleton scored in four of his next six games as United went on a twelve-match unbeaten run.

By the end of his first season at the club, Stapleton had finished United's top scorer with thirteen goals in forty-one league games, as they finished third in the league. It was the closest Stapleton would actually get to winning a league championship with United, but the team did have some excellent cup runs during his time there.

In the 1982–83 season, United beat Stapleton's old club Arsenal in both the Milk

Cup and FA Cup semi-finals. He was on the losing team in the Milk Cup final to Liverpool, but picked up an FA Cup winners' medal with victory over Brighton.

Stapleton famously scored in the 2–2 draw with Brighton in the FA Cup final at Wembley, and, in doing so, became the first player to score for two separate teams in FA Cup finals. United subsequently won the replay 4–0.

Stapleton finished the season as United's top scorer once again, with nineteen goals in all competitions.

The following year, he played a central role in one of United's best European performances for many years.

Trailing 2–0 to Barcelona after the first leg of a Cup Winners' Cup quarter-final tie, the team managed to turn the deficit around to beat the Spanish giants in front of a delighted Old Trafford crowd. After England captain Bryan Robson had scored two goals to put United 2–0 up, the stage was set for Stapleton to smash home a famous winner.

Unfortunately, Stapleton could not repeat his heroics in the semi-final as United crashed out to Juventus.

Stapleton was unable to start the 1984–85 season because of injury, and United used a new striker in the form of Welshman Mark Hughes.

Stapleton eventually came back into the side in December 1984 and picked up where he had left off by knocking in a few more crucial goals. He played a big part in helping United reach their second FA Cup final in three years, when he scored against Liverpool in their drawn semi-final clash.

Stapleton was in the United team that took to the field for the Cup final against newly crowned league champions Everton at Wembley.

Despite partnering Mark Hughes in a strong attack, neither striker was able to get on the score sheet during the ninety minutes as the game ended 0–0, with Norman Whiteside eventually winning it for United in extra time.

"It's hard to describe the welcome I got. Vociferous is one way of putting it. There was quite a bit of flak flying about but I quite enjoyed it."

Frank Stapleton, on his first return to Highbury after his bitter switch from Arsenal to United.

Stapleton remained part of the team that started the next season in record-breaking fashion as they won their first ten league games on the trot. They were unable to keep it going, however, and after only a fourth place finish in the league that year, manager Ron Atkinson was replaced by Alex Ferguson.

It wasn't long before Ferguson began to ring the changes at United and Stapleton found himself on his way out of Old Trafford, when he was sold to Dutch club Ajax in the summer of 1987.

In his six years at United, Frank Stapleton had managed to find the back of the net seventy-eight times.

*Stapleton is tackled by Liverpool's
Mark Lawrenson.*

Frank Stapleton also enjoyed an illustrious international career with the Republic of Ireland, notching up twenty goals – which had made him his country's top goal scorer until Niall Quinn and Robbie Keane surpassed that total in later years. He captained the side that made its historic first appearance at a major finals in Euro '88 and was also part of the squad that travelled to Italy for the World Cup in 1990.

Other Clubs: Arsenal, Ajax, Anderlecht, Derby County, Le Harve, Blackburn
International Record: Republic of Ireland
Caps: 71
Goals: 20

Paul McGrath	
Place of birth:	Ealing, England
Date of birth:	4 December 1959
Position:	Central defender
Years at United:	1982–1989
Games played:	199
Goals:	16
Honours:	FA Cup (1985)

There has rarely been a player who has engendered as much affection from football fans as the imperious Paul McGrath.

Known as the 'Black Pearl' from his days with League of Ireland club St Patrick's Athletic, top-class defender McGrath signed for Manchester United in 1982.

He had already come to the attention of eagle-eyed United scout Billy Behan whilst he was still playing junior football with Dalkey United in Dublin. So it was no surprise when he arrived at Old Trafford to begin a career in professional football.

McGrath made his United debut in a 1–0 home win over Tottenham in November 1982, under the watchful eye of new manager Ron Atkinson.

He was by no means a regular in the United team that season, however, appearing in only thirteen more games as Atkinson preferred to use the more experienced Scots Gordon McQueen and Martin Buchan, and McGrath's fellow Dubliner Kevin Moran.

Similar to Moran, McGrath had the happy knack of chipping in with his fair share of goals and he managed to notch up three in his debut season. United finished that season playing in both the Milk Cup and FA Cup finals, but McGrath had to settle for watching both games from the stands.

McGrath also had to bide his time during the 1983–84 season, making just fleeting appearances as United made it to the semi-finals of the European Cup Winners' Cup.

However, his magnificent natural talent, coupled with an incredible ability to read the game, meant it was only a matter of time before McGrath nailed down a permanent place in the United team.

He proved this in the 1984–85 season when he built up an excellent central defensive partnership with Moran, playing in

Paul McGrath.

McGrath tackles Gary Linekar of Everton in the 1985 Charity Shield.

Paul McGrath celebrates scoring against Liverpool in 1985.

twenty-three of United's league games that season, as they finished fourth.

Probably McGrath's best performance in a United shirt came in the 1985 FA Cup final against Everton at Wembley.

Marking the much-feared Everton striker Graeme Sharp, McGrath barely gave the Scotsman a sniff of goal all day as he helped to snuff out every Everton attack. When his partner Moran got sent-off during the game,

McGrath seemed to up his performance another notch and he was eventually named Man of the Match as United won 1–0 in extra time.

This really did prove to be McGrath's career highlight at Old Trafford, however, as the talented United team failed to win any more trophies under Ron Atkinson.

In the 1985–86 season, McGrath was almost an ever-present in the United team, playing in forty of United's forty-two leagues games and scoring three goals. But, despite a brilliant start to that season, United flattered to deceive and could only finish in fourth spot in the league.

Following a poor start to the 1986–87 campaign, United replaced Ron Atkinson with Alex Ferguson in November.

With the club languishing near the bottom of the table, Ferguson guided them to the relative safety of eleventh place by the end of the season, with McGrath appearing in thirty-one games.

However, McGrath's importance to the United team began to wane under the Ferguson regime, who took a stricter stance on the defender's wayward drinking problem and McGrath played in just twenty-two of United's league games in the 1987–88 season, as to the team finished in second place behind champions Liverpool.

He lasted one more season under Ferguson, playing twenty more league games for the Scot.

With McGrath beginning to suffer recurring knee problems, Ferguson feared the defender would have to quit the game and McGrath eventually departed Old Trafford in 1989. He moved to Aston Villa, where he overcame the problems with his knees to enjoy an inspirational career.

> "I hated Fergie at the time but I have come to understand what he did. He has been nothing but kind to me since I left the club and has shown himself to be a decent human being."

Defender Paul McGrath on his ousting from Man Utd by Sir Alex Ferguson.

McGrath's Aston Villa side even pushed United all the way in the 1992–93 season, when Ferguson finally landed his first championship success.

Versatile McGrath also played in midfield for the Republic of Ireland team that played at Euro '88 in Germany. One of the Republic of Ireland's greatest players, he maintained his place in the Irish midfield for their journey to the quarter-finals of the World Cup in 1990.

He later reverted to playing as a centre-half for Ireland and was as imperious as ever as he helped his country to a historic 1–0 victory over Italy in the World Cup in 1994, with one of his best performances.

McGrath, who was named the Professional Footballer Association (PFA) Player of the Year in 1993, also won his first trophy for Villa in 1994, defeating his old team Manchester United in the League Cup final.

Other Clubs: St Patrick's Athletic, Aston Villa, Derby County, Sheffield Utd
International Record: Republic of Ireland
Caps: 83
Goals: 8

Ten Great 'Green Devil' Goals

The old adage that any goal is a good goal rings particularly true if it happens to be the all-important winning strike in a game.

Yet, football fans will always crave the one act of genius that can turn any game on its head – whether it is a mazy run or stunning strike that has the crowd leaping with joy and wonder. Man Utd's glittering history is littered which such extraordinary moments of magic, with many of them from the boot or head of an Irishman.

Below is a sprinkling, in no particular order, of ten great Green Devils' goals.

Norman Whiteside
Manchester Utd 1–0 Everton
FA Cup final, Wembley
18 May 1985

In a game that looked like a breakthrough was never going to happen, Norman Whiteside lit up Wembley with one of the best goals ever seen in a FA Cup final.

With the game tied at 0–0 in the second half of extra time, Whiteside collected a pass from Mark Hughes and advanced from the right of midfield to the edge of the Everton box. Before any Everton defenders could make a challenge, he bent a sweet left-foot shot curling beyond the reach of Everton goalie Neville Southall into the far corner of the net.

United held on for the win and Whiteside's goal has gone down as one of the best in the club's history.

George Best
Benfica 1–5 Manchester Utd
European Cup quarter-final, Estadio de Luz
9 March 1966

The mercurial winger may be better remembered for his goal against Benfica in the European Cup final in 1968, but, two years earlier, he had scored an even better one against the same opposition.

Best inspired United to an emphatic 5–1 victory in Portugal by scoring two great goals in one of the club's best ever European performances.

His second was a real joy to behold as he collected a knockdown from striker David Herd to race past three Benfica defenders with a sudden burst of pace and calmly slot the ball past the advancing goalkeeper.

Denis Irwin
Liverpool 3–3 Manchester Utd
Premier League, Anfield
4 January 1994

Denis Irwin built up a strong reputation as a brilliant free-kick taker and few in his career came much better than this belter at Anfield.

With his United side already leading 2–0, Irwin stepped up to ping a twenty-five-yard right-foot beauty up and over the Liverpool wall to nestle in the top corner of the net.

Unfortunately for Irwin, Liverpool made an unlikely comeback to etch out a 3–3 draw.

Liam Whelan
Athletico Bilboa 5–3 Manchester Utd
European Cup quarter-final, Bilboa
21 November 1956

In a first-leg, European Cup quarter-final tie that United were losing 5–2, Liam Whelan stepped forward to score a fantastic goal with five minutes remaining in the game.

He picked the ball up deep in his own half and set off on a mazy run, which left five Bilboa defenders for dead, before slipping the ball into the net.

It proved a crucial goal as United won the second leg 3–0 to advance to the semi-finals with a 6–5 aggregate win.

Keith Gillespie
Manchester Utd 2–0 Newcastle
Premier League, Old Trafford
24 October 1994

Keith Gillespie's only league goal for Manchester United was an absolute beauty.

With United struggling to shake off Newcastle in a gritty Premier League game at Old Trafford, Gillespie unleashed an unstoppable right-foot shot from over twenty-five-yards out that flew into the top corner of the Newcastle net to secure a precious 2–0 win.

Sammy McIlroy
Manchester Utd 2–3 Arsenal
FA Cup final, Wembley
12 May 1979

It may not have won the FA Cup for United, but Sammy McIlroy's equaliser in the pulsating finish to the 1979 final at Wembley was still one to savour.

Trailing 2–0 with five minutes to go, United pulled a goal back through Gordon McQueen and, just two minutes later, McIlroy took centre stage with an exquisite goal.

He picked up the ball on the edge of the Arsenal penalty area before deftly beating two defenders with a twisting run inside the box and passing the ball past the oncoming Pat Jennings in the Arsenal goal.

Sadly for McIlroy, Arsenal's Alan Sunderland stole his thunder with a last-minute winner to break United hearts.

Roy Keane
Manchester Utd 2–0 Birmingham City
Premier League, Old Trafford
5 February 2005

Persistent injuries may well have been taking their toll on United captain Roy Keane as he neared the end of his Old Trafford career, but he still found the power and stamina to score a cracking goal against Birmingham City.

With United trying to make the breakthrough after a first-half stalemate, Keane made a bursting run to latch on to a cheeky back-heel from Christiano Ronaldo on fifty-five minutes.

He beat off the challenge of the retreating Birmingham defence before taking an extra touch on the edge of the box to crash a powerful low shot into the back of the net.

To top things off, this belting goal was Keane's fiftieth strike for Manchester United.

Norman Whiteside
Manchester Utd 2–1 Arsenal
FA Cup semi-final, Villa Park
16 April 1983

The goal that got Ron Atkinson's United to the 1983 FA Cup final was another of 'Storming Norman's' cracking goals which made him such a hero with United fans throughout the 1980s.

With this hard-fought semi-final clash tied at 1–1, Whiteside latched on to a long ball that landed just inside the Arsenal penalty area. Before Arsenal's Irish defender David O'Leary had a chance to react, seventeen-year-old Whiteside had lashed an unstoppable left-foot shot into the top corner of the Arsenal net.

Shay Brennan
Manchester Utd 3–0 Sheffield Wednesday
FA Cup, Old Trafford
19 February 1958

Making his debut for Manchester United, twenty-year-old reserve full-back Shay Brennan was brought into the side for an extremely emotional FA Cup tie with Sheffield Wednesday.

It was United's first match since the tragedy of the Munich Air Disaster and Brennan was asked to play in the unfamiliar role of outside-left. Brennan excelled that night, scoring two goals as United won 3–0.

Brennan's first goal arrived on twenty-seven minutes when he scored straight from a corner kick. Brennan floated a ball into the box that Wednesday's keeper Brian Ryalls was unable to hold on to and it ended up in the net. It was one of only six goals Brennan scored in a glittering Manchester Utd career.

George Best
Manchester Utd 4–1 Benfica
European Cup final, Wembley
29 May 1968

A crowning moment in George Best's whirlwind United career came in the 1968 European Cup final against Benfica at Wembley.

With the teams tied at 1–1 after full-time, Best took centre stage in extra time to score an excellent goal. Showing all his predatory instincts, Best latched on to a flick from a booming goal kick from United keeper Alex Stepney, to nutmeg a Benfica defender before coolly rounding the Portuguese keeper Henrique to slot the ball into an empty net.

The goal broke Benfica's resilience and United went on to capture their first European Cup.

Fans

When Manchester United celebrated their stunning Premier League and Champions League double in May 2008, the club was cheered by well over 1 million avid Irish fans.

It is an astonishing number of people to support one club in a country the size of Ireland and marks Manchester United as not only the most popular English football club on Irish shores, but also one of the country's biggest phenomenons.

Manchester United's loyal support base in Ireland is one that has developed over many decades of triumph and tragedy. From the glory and heartbreak of the Busby Babes in the 1950s, through the disaster of relegation in the mid-1970s and on to the club's stunning reinvention under Sir Alex Ferguson, Red Devils' fans in Ireland have supported the team with pride and passion.

The club's popularity has no doubt been helped by Irish footballing legends – such as Carey, Cantwell, Best and Keane – but this is by no means the only reason Manchester United is such a big entity in Ireland.

Fans old enough to remember will say it is the style of football that Manchester United has become synonymous with that first got them hooked. It was a style based on a sense of football freedom, encapsulating ingenuity and flair, which post-war manager Matt Busby always championed.

It is why, in May 1969, up to 300 Red Devils' fans packed into a hotel conference hall in Dún Laoghaire in south Dublin to establish Ireland's first ever Man Utd supporters club.

Almost forty years later, that club – The Official Manchester United Supporters Club (Ireland Branch) – is still in existence and, like Man Utd itself, is growing bigger and stronger by the year.

It has been joined by countless other fan clubs dotted all over the country and, now, there is not a county or large town in Ireland that doesn't have its own supporters branch.

A lot has happened in the four decades since the first Man Utd supporters club came into existence in Ireland and club secretary Eddie Gibbons has been there to see it all.

A Man Utd fan from the day he found out what football was all about, fifty-nine-year-old Dubliner Eddie has witnessed the club's finest moments and is one of the few Irishmen who can boast about being present at the club's three European Champions Cup triumphs.

Eddie's football memory bank is laden with colourful tales of supporting United across Europe.

He can recall sharing the train back from London to Manchester with the victorious 1968 European Cup winning team, despite the fact he was supposed to be enjoying his honeymoon with new wife Kay in Wexford. 'A group of eight of us spent two great nights in Manchester celebrating that fantastic win, until we ran out of money and some nice policemen had to escort us onto a boat back to Dublin,' he says.

A year after that momentous occasion, Eddie was one of the first to help set up the new supporters club, which now caters for over 1,000 fans.

Eddie revealed one of the fan club's biggest supporters was manager Sir Matt Busby himself. 'Sir Matt gave the club great help and advice when setting up and always ensured there were tickets available for any game we wished to go to. Even for any of the really big games, Sir Matt would make sure we got up to 300 to 400 tickets if needed. To this day, Sir Matt remains the supporters club's Honorary President because of all the help and support he has given the club.'

Throughout all the success Eddie and the supporters club have enjoyed during their time following Man Utd, he can also recall the dark period of relegation in 1974.

But even in this, the United fanatic finds a silver lining.

'Some of the football the team played during their year in the Second Division during 1974–75 was some of the most enjoyable in the club's history,' he says. 'There were some great games that year, when the team attacked and scored plenty of goals and fully deserved to be promoted straight back up as winners of the division.'

Supporting United at the 2007 FA Cup semi-final.

Even after this, it took Man Utd a further eighteen years to win back the league championship crown and, true to form, Eddie was there on the night they finally did it.

'The night Manchester United beat Blackburn at Old Trafford to clinch the league title in 1993 was a very emotional occasion; it was a marvellous night which many of us just couldn't see happening for so many years.'

As the supporters club nears its fortieth year in 2009, it will be joined by Sir Alex Ferguson and great club stalwarts Ryan Giggs and Paul Scholes to celebrate the occasion in Dublin.

Eddie says such occasions are recognition from the big names at the club of the vitally important role played by the fans. 'I believe it is their way of saying thank you to the fans and recognising all the hard work we do in supporting the team. We spend a lot of our money and time travelling around in support of Man Utd and it is great to know that this is appreciated by the coaches and players at the club.'

Roy Keane celebrates winning the 2003 Premier League.

The Ferguson Era

(1986-present)

When Alex Ferguson strode into Manchester United in November 1986, he found a club in desperate need of a new saviour. It had been almost twenty years since the heady days of the 1960s, when Matt Busby was manager and when the club had last tasted league glory.

As the latest incumbent in Busby's throne, Ferguson was left in no doubt about what was required when he arrived at Old Trafford from Scottish club Aberdeen.

The fiery Scot had built up a reputation as a stern but successful manager with the Dons, guiding them to three Scottish League titles and had even enjoyed a European Cup Winners' Cup triumph.

All of this meant very little when he came to United, however, as Ferguson laid his reputation on the line in a bid to reignite the sleeping giant of Manchester. Set against this backdrop, Ferguson also had to deal with a pervasive drinking culture that had been apparent amongst some of United's more senior players for some time. But rather than making any wholesale changes, Ferguson gradually went about transforming the United team into his style and liking.

He decided against making any moves in the transfer market during his first season at the club. Instead, he concentrated on guiding United away from the relegation zone and they finished the 1986–87 in eleventh place in the league.

Having secured a top-half finish, Ferguson had learned enough about his team to start making changes. In the summer of 1987, he snapped up defender Steve Bruce from Norwich City and forward Brian McClair from Glasgow Celtic, paying over £800,000 for each player – and both would go on to prove excellent value for money in the long term.

Meanwhile, Ferguson also allowed top Irish striker Frank Stapleton to leave the club, along with goalkeeper Gary Bailey and forward Terry Gibson.

With Irish defenders Kevin Moran and Paul McGrath and forward Norman Whiteside

Alex Ferguson joined United in 1986 and has become the club's most successful manager.

still part of his plans, Ferguson's new-look United side had a very impressive league campaign during 1987–88 as they finished runners-up to Liverpool.

That summer, Ferguson brought in top Scottish goalkeeper Jim Leighton, striker Mark Hughes, defender Mal Donaghy and young winger Lee Sharpe in the hope that his team could go one better than the previous year. Instead, they appeared to go backwards and finished eleventh in the league.

Despite this, Ferguson was given the full backing of the United board as he went on a major spending spree in the summer of 1989, signing Gary Pallister, Paul Ince, Neil Webb and Danny Wallace, all for big money.

As well as this Ferguson allowed fans' favourites Paul McGrath and Norman Whiteside to leave the club. It was a gamble that appeared to backfire as many of Ferguson's new signings failed to live up to their initial expectations and United could only finish thirteenth in the league in 1990, but Ferguson was spared the sack by leading the team into their first FA Cup final in five years.

United eventually overcame Crystal Palace 1–0 in a replay to capture the Cup and Ferguson used the momentum gained from this to really press on with the team. He made some shrewd signings that year, such as Denis Irwin for the senior team and a youngster by the name of Ryan Giggs came to the club to play in the youth side.

Winning the FA Cup gave United a place in the European Cup Winners' Cup in 1991 and Ferguson led the team to an eagerly awaited final against Spanish giants Barcelona. United

Mark Hughes lifts the European Cup Winners' Cup after a scoring both goals in a 2–1 victory over Barcelona.

were on top form on the night with frontman Mark Hughes scoring twice as the Red Devils captured the cup in a 2–1 win.

This European triumph lifted United onto another level and, with Liverpool losing their grip as the most dominant team in England, Ferguson sensed the chance was there to bring United back to the very top.

Another final followed in 1992, when United overcame Nottingham Forest 1–0 in the Rumbelows League Cup final. However, for all the recent success, it was the league title that everyone at Old Trafford really craved and there was a huge sense of hurt at the club when they missed out on it to Leeds Utd in 1992.

United players celebrate winning the league after a twenty-six-year wait.

Nevertheless, United's growing presence at the top of the league could not be ignored.

With the advent of Sky Sports and the new Premier League taking the place of the old First Division at the beginning of the 1992–93 season, top-flight football in England was moving to a higher plane.

Ferguson ensured Manchester Utd were at the very heart of this as he made what was possibly his most significant move in the transfer market by prising French forward Eric Cantona away from rivals Leeds Utd.

The other players to arrive at Old Trafford were Danish goalkeeper Peter Schmeichel and flying winger Andrei Kanchelskis.

Ferguson now had the basis for a league-title winning team and United finally ended their chronic twenty-six-year wait by landing the Premier League crown in May 1993.

The victory was just rewards for those on the United board who had stuck by Ferguson for six years when it would have seemed easier to have sacked him.

In his relentless search for more glory, Ferguson shelled out £3.75 million to bring Irish midfielder Roy Keane to Old Trafford in the summer of 1993. It proved to be an inspired purchase as the midfielder would help bring United to an even higher level of brilliance.

United retained their Premier League title in 1994 as it became apparent that, in

Liverpool's absence, they had become the unstoppable force in English football.

They added to their league title with the FA Cup, following a 4–0 win over Chelsea at Wembley, ensuring Ferguson hero status almost on a par with Busby.

United's success and growing popularity meant the club also had to devise plans to expand Old Trafford. The fabled ground, dubbed the 'Theatre of Dreams' by United legend Bobby Charlton, had seen its capacity reduced to just 40,000 by the mid-1990s due to the banishment of standing terraces in favour of all-seater stadia.

As Old Trafford had also being earmarked to host a number of important games during Euro '96, the club decided to take action. Construction on a brand new north stand

began in 1995, bringing it as high as three tiers and raising the capacity at Old Trafford to 55,000, giving United the biggest ground in the Premier League.

While league titles and FA cups continued to come United's way during the 1990s, Ferguson's obsession turned to emulating Busby by winning the European Cup.

Like Busby, Ferguson had set about establishing one of the best youth systems in the country, when he signed a host of extremely talented players from a young age. David Beckham, Ryan Giggs, Paul Scholes, Nicky Butt and Gary and Phil Neville all came through United's youth cup winning side of the early 1990s to make an impact in the first team.

Ferguson had such confidence in this

Old Trafford's redeveloped North Stand, 1996.

After the most dramatic of finishes, United players celebrate winning the 1999 European Champions League.

new batch of youngsters that he even allowed top senior players like Paul Ince, Andrei Kanchelskis and Mark Hughes to leave the club in 1995.

Ferguson's gamble paid off once again as his new-look United side captured a second double in three years in 1996.

A year later, United marched on to the semi-finals of the European Champions League, before bowing out to eventual winners Borussia Dortmund. It was a crushing blow for Ferguson, but he remained determined to get United into the final.

After losing their league title to Arsenal in 1998, Ferguson's United came back stronger than ever to claim the league and cup double in 1999.

Ferguson also guided his talented side to the holy grail of a European Champions League final that year, when they played German giants Bayern Munich in an unforgettable match in Barcelona.

Despite missing top midfielders Roy Keane and Paul Scholes through suspension, United won the final 2–1 with two dramatic last gasp goals from strikers Teddy Sheringham and Ole Gunnar Solksjaer. The win elevated Ferguson to the position as United's most successful manager, and he was even knighted for his services to the game of football following this achievement.

By the turn of the century, Irish interest in the club had also grown in the form of horse racing tycoons J.P. McManus and John Magnier. Between them, the millionaire Irishmen had snapped up almost a 30 per cent stake in the club's shares, making them two of the more prominent shareholders at the club.

Old Trafford also continued to expand, with a second tier added to both the ground's East and West piers in 2001, bringing the capacity up to just over 68,000.

In the meantime, Ferguson (now known as Sir Alex) managed to lead United to another two league titles in 2000 and 2001, but they could not repeat their 1999 Champions League success.

Mindful of this, Ferguson splashed out over £45 million on Dutch striker Ruud van Nistelroy and Argentinian midfielder Juan Sebastian Veron in the summer of 2001 with the hope United would win back their European crown.

Whilst Van Nistelroy proved a huge hit with the fans by scoring numerous important goals for the club, United were still unable to recapture the Champions League. They did win back their league crown in 2003, but the excellence of their old adversaries Arsenal and the emergence of a very strong Chelsea side meant the trophy was kept away from Old Trafford for the next three years.

By 2005, however, significant events off the pitch threatened to ruin United's strong association with their loyal fan base.

J.P. McManus and John Magnier decided to sell their major share in United to American tycoon Malcolm Glazer, who was attempting to gain sole ownership of the club. Glazer eventually succeeded in this aim, which angered many staunch Man Utd supporters who did not want the club taken over by this one man.

Nevertheless, United returned to their successful ways on the pitch after this, as Ferguson found renewed energy for the battle. Rather than retire while the going was good, Ferguson decided to take the Chelsea challenge head-on and has amazingly brought United back to the very top of the tree.

He made some astute new signings in the form of young Portuguese winger Christiano Ronaldo and English forward Wayne Rooney,

Fans show their disapproval of the takeover by Malcolm Glazer.

as well as strengthening his defence with Serbian centre-half Nemanja Vidic and French full-back Patrice Evra.

The result was that United regained their league title in 2007 and added a phenomenal tenth championship crown under Ferguson's reign at the end of the 2007–08 season.

To top if off, United also captured their third European Cup by beating Chelsea in a penalty shootout in the 2008 Champions League final.

As if to fully emphasise their dominance on the English game in the past two decades, United have continued to expand the impressive Old Trafford, which can now hold a capacity of over 70,000 people – far more than any of their rivals.

Sir Alex Ferguson remains on as the United manager, where, true to form, he will be aiming to add more silverware to Old Trafford's bulging trophy cabinet.

Hat-tricks

Since the beginning of association football, a player scoring three goals in the one game has always been a much feted accomplishment.

The term 'hat-trick' – borrowed from the game of cricket – became the goal-scoring exploit all forwards strove to achieve.

The art of scoring hat-tricks is one that most of Manchester United's top marksmen have perfected, right through from Newton Heath's goal getter Bob Donaldson to 1960s legend Denis Law and Dutch striker Ruud van Nistelroy.

Irish players at the club have not been shy on the hat-trick front either, with wing-wizard George Best famously scoring a double hat-trick during an FA Cup tie with Northampton Town.

Best aside, other Irishmen have also etched their name into the club's record books since Liam Whelan first notched up three in a game in 1957.

Below is a list of hat-tricks scored for Manchester United by the club's very own Green Devils' three-goal heroes.

4 April 1957
Burnley 1–3 Manchester Utd   Liam Whelan (3)

24 August 1957
Leicester City 0–3 Manchester Utd   Liam Whelan (3)

4 May 1968
Manchester Utd 6–0 Newcastle Utd   George Best (3)

7 February 1970
Northampton Town 2–8 Manchester Utd   George Best (6)

18 September 1971
Manchester Utd 4–2 West Ham   George Best (3)

27 November 1971
Southampton 2–5 Manchester Utd

George Best (3)

24 August 1974
Manchester Utd 4–0 Millwall

Gerry Daly (3)

3 October 1981
Manchester Utd 5–0 Wolves

Sammy McIlroy (3)

19 November 1983
Manchester Utd 4–1 Watford

Frank Stapleton (3)

9 March 1985
Manchester Utd 4–2 West Ham

Norman Whiteside (3)

Player Profiles

Derek Brazil	
Place of birth:	Belfast
Date of birth:	14 December 1968
Position:	Defender
Years at United:	1986–1992
Games played:	2
Goals:	0

Derek Brazil arrived at Old Trafford in March 1986, when Ron Atkinson's charges were still chasing that elusive league title.

Arriving from schoolboy club Rivermount Boys, the eighteen-year-old defender didn't have far to look for advice, as fellow Dubliners Kevin Moran and Paul McGrath were the mainstays in the United defence at the time.

Young Brazil played for a couple of years in the United reserve team and was capped by the Republic of Ireland at all levels up to B International.

His breakthrough into the United first team didn't arrive until May 1989, when Ferguson played him in a home game against Everton. United lost that match 2–1, and Brazil only featured in one more game at Old Trafford before he was sent out on loan to Welsh club Swansea City in September 1991.

Brazil made twelve appearances for Swansea during that season and even managed to pitch in with a goal.

On his return to Manchester United, he was sold to Cardiff City in August 1992 in a deal worth £85,000. Brazil starred in the Cardiff team that went to win the English Third Division title in 1992–93 and also managed to pick up a Welsh Cup winners' medal during his time there.

Other Clubs: Rivermount Boys, Oldham, Swansea, Cardiff

Top Ten Green Devils Appearances

1. Tony Dunne – 535
2. Denis Irwin – 529
3. Roy Keane – 480
4. George Best – 470
5. Sammy McIlroy – 419
6. Shay Brennan – 359
7. Johnny Carey – 344
8. John O'Shea – 298 (still playing)
9. Kevin Moran – 289
10. Frank Stapleton – 288

Liam O'Brien	
Place of birth:	Dublin
Date of birth:	5 September 1964
Position:	Midfielder
Years at United:	1986–1988
Games played:	36
Goals:	2

Midfielder Liam O'Brien was signed by Manchester United manager Ron Atkinson from Shamrock Rovers for £50,000 in October 1987. It was the last major transfer deal that Big Ron would make as, just a month later, he was let go without O'Brien playing a game for him.

O'Brien's United debut eventually arrived under new boss Sir Alex Ferguson, when he played in a 2–0 win over Leicester City at Old Trafford on 20 December 1986.

His next start came in a 4–1 win over Newcastle Utd on New Year's Day 1987, but, overall, O'Brien's chances at the club were fairly limited. United were already blessed with excellent options in midfield, such as Bryan Robson and Gordon Strachan, and the elegant O'Brien often found himself being used as a substitute.

Nevertheless, he helped to steer United away from the relegation zone into the relative comfort of eleventh place, as he played in nine league games that season.

United mounted a much better challenge in the league the following season, eventually finishing runners-up to Liverpool, but O'Brien

found himself being used mostly from the bench.

The highlight of O'Brien's career at the club came when he scored the winner in a 1–0 win over Coventry at Old Trafford on 6 February 1988 – which was poignant as it was the thirtieth anniversary of the Munich Air Disaster.

A month later, he notched up his second goal for United in a 2–1 win over Chelsea but, despite the occasional start, O'Brien was still used mainly as a substitute.

On the international front, O'Brien travelled to Germany with the Republic of

Ireland side that qualified for Euro '88. However, with Irish manager Jack Charlton having an embarrassment of riches in midfield, O'Brien did not make it into the side that almost qualified for the semi-finals.

When O'Brien failed to claim a regular first-team place with United the following season, he was eventually sold on to Newcastle Utd for £275,000.

His last game for United came in a 1–1 draw at home to Aston Villa on 5 November 1988.

Other Clubs: Bohemians, Shamrock Rovers, Newcastle Utd, Tranmere Rovers, Cork City
International Record: Republic of Ireland
Caps: 16
Goals: 0

Mal Donaghy	
Place of birth:	Belfast
Date of birth:	13 September 1957
Position:	Defender
Years at United:	1988–1992
Games played:	119
Goals:	0
Honours:	Cup Winners' Cup (1991)

There aren't many players who begin their Manchester United careers having already spent almost ten years at the top, but versatile Northern Ireland defender Mal Donaghy signed for Alex Ferguson's Man Utd in 1988, having already given a decade of sterling service to Luton Town.

He was brought in to help strengthen a defence that had just lost Irish stalwart Kevin Moran.

Donaghy could play equally as well at either right-back or central defence and became an important figure in the United rearguard.

He had also already starred in two World Cups for Northern Ireland in 1982 and 1986 and became his county's most capped outfield player during a fourteen-year international career.

He made his debut for Manchester United in a 1–1 draw away to Everton in October 1988 and was a virtual ever-present for the rest of the season.

United struggled that year, however, and finished only eleventh in the league, but the following season sparked the beginning of United's massive revival of fortunes under Ferguson.

Donaghy started the 1989–90 season in the United side, but, after an indifferent couple of months, which included a 5–1 derby day hammering by Manchester City, he was loaned out to his old club Luton Town.

After playing five games for Luton, Donaghy returned to Old Trafford, where he helped United edge past minnows Hereford Utd with a 1–0 win on their way to capturing the FA Cup.

It was the only FA Cup tie Donaghy started that year, as his role in the United side became increasingly limited.

Mal Donaghy.

Donaghy's next appearance was at Wembley the following August, as Man Utd began their season with a 1–1 draw in the Charity Shield against Liverpool.

With United embarking on a momentous European Cup Winners' Cup campaign, Donaghy found himself in the side a lot more because of the extra games United had to play.

He played in twenty-five league games that year and also helped United to the final of the Cup Winners' Cup with wins over French club Montpellier and Poland's Legia Warsaw in the semi-final. Although Donaghy was an unused sub in the final, he picked up a winners' medal as United overcame Barcelona 2–1.

It was the highlight of Donaghy's time at Old Trafford, although he did spend another season at the club as United won the Rumbelows League Cup and finished second to Leeds Utd in the league.

Donaghy played in twenty league games during the 1991–92 season, before being sold to Chelsea in August 1992.

His last game for United came in a 3–1 win over Tottenham at Old Trafford.

Other Clubs: Larne, Luton Town, Chelsea
International Record: Northern Ireland
Caps: 91
Goals: 0

Denis Irwin	
Place of birth:	Cork
Date of birth:	31 October 1965
Position:	Right/left full-back
Years at United:	1990–2002
Games played:	529
Goals:	33
Honours:	Premier League (1993, 1994, 1996, 1997, 1999, 2000, 2001); FA Cup (1994, 1996, 1999); League Cup (1992); Cup Winners' Cup (1991); Champions League (1999)

When twenty-four-year-old Denis Irwin made the short move from Oldham Athletic to Manchester United in 1990, he could scarcely have believed the glittering career that lay ahead for him.

Alex Ferguson's United had just been crowned FA Cup winners but quiet Corkman Irwin arrived at just the time things really started to take off for the club.

A consummate professional, Irwin could play equally as well at either right- or left-back, and he rarely had a bad game during his twelve-year Old Trafford career. As well as being able to defend incredibly well, Irwin was also more than capable of bombing forward down the wings to launch attacks. To add to his armoury, he possessed a deadly right-foot shot that he used to great affect down the years taking both free kicks and penalties.

185

Alex Ferguson Era (1986–present)

Irwin's first job when he arrived at United was to help the team into the European Cup Winners' Cup final in 1991 – the club's first major European final in twenty-three years.

As a sign of things to come, United beat Barcelona 2–1 that night, with Irwin going about his job with the minimum of fuss.

During his second season with the club, Irwin appeared in another Cup final, as the Red Devils overcame Nottingham Forest 1–0 at Wembley to claim the Rumbelows League Cup.

Irwin did suffer the pain of losing out on the league championship crown, however, when his highly fancied United team were pipped to the First Division title by an Eric Cantona-inspired Leeds Utd.

Man Utd weren't to be denied the following season, though, when after snapping up Cantona from Leeds, Alex Ferguson's team ended the club's agonising twenty-six-year wait for a league title. Denis Irwin was an ever-present during that momentous season, playing in all of United's forty league games and pitching in with five crucial goals.

By now, Irwin was playing mostly as a left-back to accommodate England's Paul Parker on the right of the United defence.

The following season, Irwin was a key member in the United side that claimed the club's first league and FA Cup double. Once again, he had an exemplary appearance record that season, playing in every one of United's forty-two league games as they coasted to the Premier League crown.

Irwin also played at the 1994 World Cup with the Republic of Ireland and is regarded as one of the best full-backs to have ever played for the country.

As United continued to mop up trophies throughout the 1990s, Irwin was there for every minute of it, ensuring that not only was he now the best full-back in the Premier Division but also the most decorated. He added a second league and FA Cup double in 1996 and his fourth league winners' medal came a year later in 1997.

> "I know I don't get any headlines, but I'll leave that to the forwards, because when the stick is being dished out they're usually first in line as well"
>
> **Denis Irwin, explaining the secret to his success.**

But the best was yet to come.

Irwin was an integral part of the United team that marched forward on three fronts during the 1998–99 season.

He played an absolutely crucial role in ensuring United progressed in the league, FA Cup and Champions League, by bravely stepping up to take on the responsibility of taking penalties. Of the five penalty kicks United got that season, cool-headed Irwin took four – and slotted them all home.

The only blotch during this magnificent season was a cruel red card that he picked up in a game at Anfield against Liverpool. Already on a yellow card, Irwin was harshly

Denis Irwin.

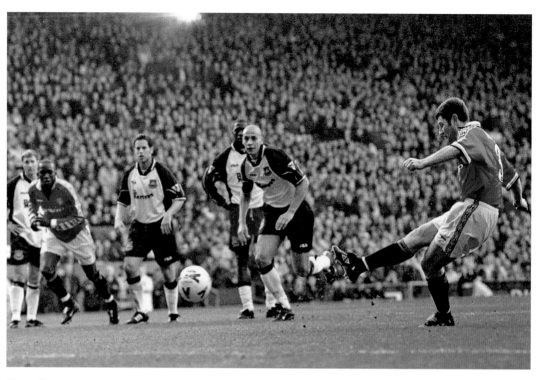

Denis Irwin scoring another penalty for United.

judged to have deliberately kicked the ball into the crowd to waste time and was given his marching orders. The sending off meant Irwin missed out on United's 2–0 FA Cup final win over Newcastle at Wembley – a win that wrapped up the club's third double under Ferguson.

Irwin was straight back on the teamsheet for United's next encounter just four days later – the historic last gasp Champions League final win over Bayern Munich.

Despite being thirty-three, Irwin continued to play on for United with his usual remarkable consistency. Wisely, manager Sir Alex began to rest him on occasions, but he was still there when called upon for the big games.

Irwin played in twenty-five of United's league games in the 1999–2000 season – as the club retained the title – scoring three goals.

The following season, he added another league winners' medal, but starred in only twenty-one games as his career at United began to wind down.

He played in just twelve games during the 2001–02 season as United lost their league title to resurgent Arsenal and was eventually let go to Wolves on a free transfer in July 2002.

Before his departure, Irwin was honoured with a testimonial game at Old Trafford against United's old rivals Manchester City.

Denis Irwin currently lies eighth in

Manchester United's appearances list – just one place below Irish full-back legend Tony Dunne – and is regarded by many as Manchester United's best ever full-back.

Other Clubs: Leeds Utd, Oldham Athletic, Wolves
International Record: Republic of Ireland
Caps: 56
Goals: 4

Pat McGibbon	
Place of birth:	Armagh
Date of birth:	6 September 1973
Position:	Central defender
Years at United:	1992–1997
Games played:	1
Goals:	0

Defender Pat McGibbon joined Manchester United in 1992, just as Alex Ferguson was turning the club into the most dominant in England. He was signed for £100,000 from Irish League side Portadown, where he had started his professional football career in 1991.

At just nineteen years of age, McGibbon found it difficult to break in to a United defence that already consisted of club legends Steve Bruce and Gary Pallister. United won back to back Premier League titles in 1993 and 1994 but McGibbon didn't play any part in the success, instead he gained experience in the reserves.

McGibbon finally made his debut for United in September 1995, in a League Cup tie with York City, when he partnered Gary Pallister in the centre of defence, in a strong-

looking United rearguard that also included Paul Parker and Denis Irwin. Despite this, United were humbled 3–0 by York City at Old Trafford.

It was the only game McGibbon ever featured in for United and despite being on the substitutes' bench on a number of occasions, he never made it on to the pitch.

In 1996, McGibbon was loaned out to Swansea to gain some first-team experience.

On his return to United in 1997, he was loaned out to Wigan Athletic, where he made a great impression and was signed permanently to the club in July 1997 for £250,000.

Other Clubs: Portadown, Wigan Athletic, Swansea City, Scunthorpe Utd, Tranmere Rovers, Glentoran
International Record: Northern Ireland
Caps: 7
Goals: 0

Roy Keane	
Place of birth:	Cork
Date of birth:	10 August 1971
Position:	Midfielder
Years at United:	1993–2005
Games played:	480
Goals:	51
Honours:	Premier League (1994, 1996, 1997, 1999, 2000, 2001, 2003); FA Cup (1994, 1996, 1999, 2004); Champions League (1999)

Regarded as one of the best midfielders of his generation, Corkman Roy Keane signed for Manchester United from Nottingham Forest in 1993 for a then British record transfer fee of £3.75 million. He arrived at Old Trafford having just suffered the ignominy of relegation with Notts Forest, but he would soon put that behind him to enjoy a period of unprecedented success with his new club.

Despite the record transfer fee on his head, twenty-two-year-old Keane still faced the tough challenge of breaking into a United midfield, which already included England legend Bryan Robson and the impressive Paul Ince – both of whom had been an integral part in the club's championship success the previous season, the first in twenty-six years.

However, typical of his career as a whole, Keane took this challenge head on and quickly set about establishing himself in the first team.

On his home debut, Keane made an instant impact by scoring twice against Sheffield Utd in a 3–0 win, thus ensuring his new-found status as an idol amongst the Old Trafford faithful. By the end of his first full season at Manchester, the combative midfielder had helped United clinch a second successive Premier League title.

He was also a key member of the team that dismantled Chelsea 4–0 in the FA Cup final at Wembley to claim a prestigious first double for the club.

Keane's second season at the club was a little less successful, however, as United suffered the pain of losing their championship crown to Kenny Dalglish's Blackburn on the last day of the season, and, a week later, Keane

> "Away from home our fans are fantastic, I'd call them the hardcore fans. But at home they have a few drinks and probably the prawn sandwiches and they don't realise what's going on out on the pitch. I don't think some of the people who come to Old Trafford can spell football, nevermind understand it."

Roy Keane, hardly endearing himself to a section of the Old Trafford support.

was in the United side that was beaten 1–0 by Everton in the FA Cup final.

United's FA Cup run that season also heralded the first of the eleven red cards Keane was to pick during his tempestuous Old Trafford career. He was sent off for stamping on Crystal Palace's Gareth Southgate during the FA Cup semi-final replay clash at Villa Park.

Nevertheless, Keane's reputation as one of the most influential players in the English game was growing by the year.

His importance to Ferguson's team was underlined the following season, when the United manager was prepared to sell Paul Ince in the summer of 1995 and make Keane his main midfield lynchpin.

That season, Keane helped a young United

side to a second double in three seasons, including a memorable 1–0 FA Cup victory against Liverpool in which he was named Man of the Match.

Keane added to his impressive medals tally with another Premier League crown in 1997, when United also showed signs they could eventually succeed in Europe. The team came agonisingly close to making the European Champions League final in 1997, only to bow out at the semi-final stage to German side Borussia Dortmund.

A suspension had kept Keane out of the United side for the crucial second leg at Old Trafford – when his presence in mid-field could have made all the difference.

Keane's rise to prominence at Man Utd was confirmed at the beginning of the 1997–98 season, when he was named club captain following the shock retirement of French icon Eric Cantona. However, his first season as captain was cut short after just two months, when he suffered an injury in the game against rivals Leeds Utd.

Keane had to be carried off the pitch on a stretcher, after rupturing his cruciate ligament following a mistimed tackle on Leeds' Norwegian midfielder Alf Inge Haaland. The injury kept Keane out for the rest of the season at the end of which United lost their Premier League title to Arsenal.

'It was the most emphatic display of selflessness I have seen on a football field. Pounding over every blade of grass, competing if he would rather die of exhaustion than lose, he inspired all around him. I felt it was an honour to be associated with such a player.'

Sir Alex Ferguson, on Keane's 1999 performance against Juventus.

Following his year out from the game, Keane was back fit and rearing to go for the 1998–99 campaign, and he could hardly have enjoyed a more successful season. He was the dynamic force behind most of United's best performances that year, as they marched on to claim a third Premier League and FA Cup double.

More importantly, however, United had finally managed to crack Europe, as Keane led them to their first European Champion's League final since their famous 1968 European Cup win.

Unfortunately for Keane, a yellow card picked up in the second leg of United's dramatic semi-final victory over Italy's Juventus meant that he was suspended for his team's historic 2–1 victory over Bayern Munich in the final. Ironically, many observers felt Keane's performance in the semi-final, when he helped drag the team back from two goals down to win 3–2, was his best ever in a red shirt.

Keane put the personal disappointment of missing out on the Champions League final behind him to lead United on to more glory in the following two seasons.

In 1999–2000, he scored two late goals in a crucial league game against Arsenal, which went a long way to keeping the Premier League trophy at Old Trafford.

Keane ended that season by claiming the

Roy Keane playing a superb game against Juventus, 1999.

double honour of being named the Professional Footballer Association (PFA) Player of the Year and the Football Writers' Player of the Year.

A year later, Keane picked up another Premier League winners' medal after United strolled to the title, finishing a comfortable ten points clear of nearest rivals Arsenal. However, Keane's fiery temper landed him in trouble again towards the end of that season when he was red-carded for a dangerous, high tackle on Alf Inge Haaland in the Manchester derby.

Injuries and suspensions began to blight Keane during the 2001–02 season, when United could only finish third in the league and ended the year without a trophy.

His troubles continued into the following season, when he received another red card for elbowing former Irish international team-mate Jason McAteer in the face during a game against Sunderland. Keane's three-game suspension for that offence was added to by a further five-game ban for an admission that his horror tackle on Haaland in the Manchester derby eighteen-months previously had been premeditated.

Keane used this time off to receive surgery on a troublesome hip injury and eventually came back into the United side in December 2002.

Despite the worrying injury, Keane had lost none of his old spark and he was back to his best as he led United to their seventh

Roy Keane celebrates another goal for United with his team-mates, 2005.

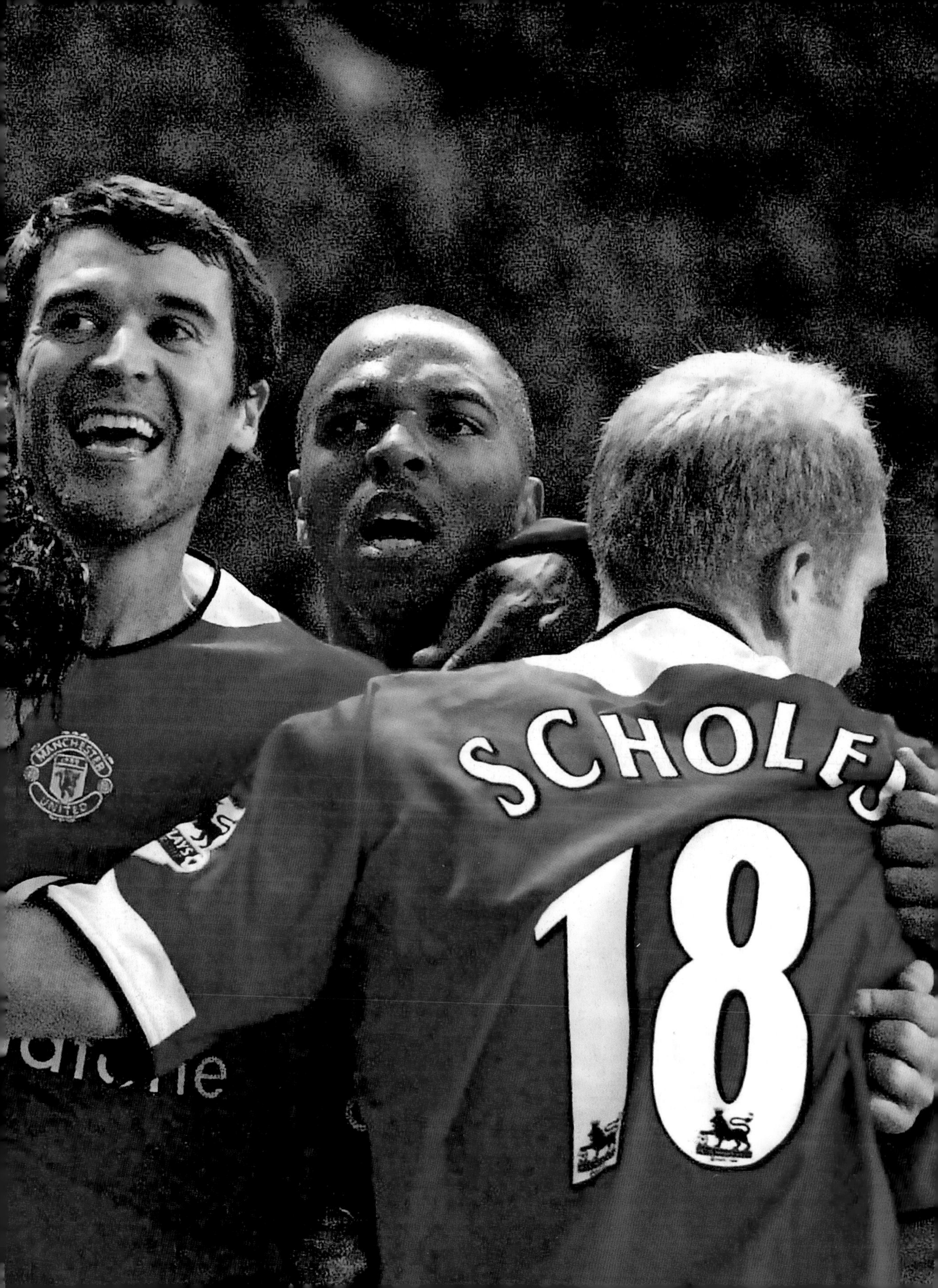
SCHOLE
18

Roy Keane salutes the crowd at the end of his testimonial match.

league title in just ten seasons in May 2003.

This proved to be the last league winners' medal Keane was to receive during his illustrious playing career, although he did add another FA Cup winners' medal in 2004.

Keane's time at United came to an abrupt end in November 2005, when an outburst on the club's official television channel MUTV led to a bitter bust-up with Sir Alex Ferguson. Keane departed the club on 18 November 2005, after twelve years of magnificent success.

A month later, he signed to play for Scottish giants Glasgow Celtic.

Roy Keane's international career with the Republic of Ireland was every bit as turbulent as his time with United.

He was one of Ireland's best players at the World Cup in 1994, as manager Jack Charlton's charges made it to the last sixteen.

Keane did more than any player to help Ireland to their third World Cup finals appearance in 2002 with magnificent performances against the mighty Portugal and Holland. However, a furious argument with manager Mick McCarthy in the lead up to the start of that World Cup whilst the team was still in training in Saipan saw Keane removed from the squad without even playing a game at the finals.

Despite his acrimonious departure from Manchester United, Keane was back at Old Trafford on 9 May 2006, where he was honoured with a testimonial game, that saw his new club Celtic play United. The game attracted a capacity crowd of 69,591, which remains the largest crowd ever for a testimonial game in England.

Roy Keane has proved to be Manchester United's most successful captain of all time, leading the club to no less than nine major honours. He was also inducted into the English Football Hall of Fame in 2004, in recognition of his impact and achievements as United captain.

Other Clubs: Cobh Ramblers, Nottingham Forest, Celtic
International Record: Republic of Ireland
Caps: 65
Goals: 9

Keith Gillespie	
Place of birth:	Antrim
Date of birth:	18 February 1975
Position:	Winger
Years at United:	1991–1995
Games played:	14
Goals:	2

When Keith Gillespie arrived at Manchester United in 1991 as a talented teenager, many at Old Trafford must have wondered if they had finally found the heir apparent to the wondrous George Best.

The fact that he came from Northern Ireland and was a pacey winger with an eye for goal made the comparisons to Best easy to understand. And, like Best, Gillespie began his United career playing in a magnificent

youth set-up and seemed destined to take his talents to new heights in the United first team.

Playing in the same side that produced David Beckham, Gary Neville, Ryan Giggs and Nicky Butt and which was considered the club's best since the Busby Babes, Gillespie won an FA Youth Cup winners' medal in 1992.

While Giggs began to make his name in the first team, Gillespie continued to shine for the youth side in 1993, as they again made it to the FA Youth Cup final. This time United were on the wrong end of a 4–1 aggregate defeat to Leeds Utd, but this did little to halt Gillespie's progress at Old Trafford.

Gillespie made his full United debut in a FA Cup clash against Bury in January 1993 and even got on the score sheet in a 2–0 win. His next outing was in another home FA Cup game, when United overcame Burnley 1–0.

Despite this promising start, Gillespie was loaned out to Wigan during the 1993–94 season in order to gain some first-team experience. Whilst there, he managed an excellent scoring ratio of four goals in just eight games and returned to Old Trafford with high hopes of claiming a permanent place in the United first-team squad.

Gillespie starred in two League Cup games against Port Vale, and United won both, and he finally made his Premier League debut in a 1–0 loss to Sheffield Wednesday in October 1994.

Gillespie's brightest moment at United came in a top of the table clash against Newcastle Utd, when he smashed home a brilliant goal in a 2–0 win. However, his chances at United remained limited and he made just nine appearances in total for the club that year.

Then, in January 1995, Sir Alex Ferguson made the bold move of signing up Newcastle's scoring sensation Andy Cole, with Gillespie moving in the opposite direction as part of the deal. Rumour has it that Ferguson was initially reluctant to lose Gillespie and only relented because of the foreigner rule that was in place at the time. Whatever the reason, the move meant Gillespie's career at United was over before it really got the chance to get going.

He did go on to enjoy some memorable moments with Newcastle in the European Champions League and has been an excellent servant to Northern Ireland.

Gillespie continues to ply his trade with Sheffield Utd in the Championship.

Other Clubs: Wigan, Newcastle Utd, Blackburn, Leicester City, Sheffield Utd
International Record: Northern Ireland
Caps: 83 (still playing)
Goals: 2

Phil Mulryne	
Place of birth:	Belfast
Date of birth:	1 January 1978
Position:	Midfielder
Years at United:	1996–1999
Games played:	5
Goals:	0

Belfast-born midfielder Phil Mulryne arrived at Manchester United as a sixteen-year-old in 1994, at a time when the club was producing some of its best youth players of all time.

With the senior team winning every thing before them in the mid-1990s and a conveyor belt of young players making the move up to Alex Ferguson's side, Mulryne had to bide his time to get a chance in United's first team. In fact, he had made his full international debut for Northern Ireland before appearing in a first team game for Manchester United.

Mulryne's debut for the Red Devils eventually arrived in October 1997, when a weakened United side lost 2–0 to Ipswich in the League Cup.

Such was the strength of the regular United midfield at the time that Mulryne rarely got an opportunity to play for the team, aside from the odd cup game.

His next appearance for United came as a substitute in a 5–1 romp over Walsall in an FA Cup at Old Trafford in January 1998.

The 1997–98 season wasn't such a great campaign for United as, shorn of their inspirational captain Roy Keane through injury, they lost their Premier League crown to Arsenal and failed to win a trophy of any kind. Mulryne played in one league game for United that season, when he started in midfield in a 2–0 win over Barnsley in an end of season game in May 1998.

It was to be the only league appearance Mulryne would make during his United career, as Alex Ferguson preferred only to play him in cup games. He was part of the United team that beat local rivals Bury 2–0 in a League Cup game at Old Trafford in October 1998, but was unable to force his way into Alex Ferguson's star-studded team.

Mulryne made just one more appearance for United, as the Red Devils beat Notts Forest 2–1 in the League Cup in November 1998.

The 1998–99 season proved to be one of United's greatest ever – winning the Premier League, FA Cup and Champions League treble – but Mulryne failed to play any part of it. The young Northern Ireland midfielder had been a victim of United's incredible success and wealth of talent at the club and was eventually sold to Norwich City in February 1999 for £500,000.

The Red Devils won four of the five games that Mulryne featured in during his five years at the club.

Other Clubs: Norwich City, Cardiff City, Leyton Orient
International Record: Northern Ireland
Caps: 27
Goals: 3

Roy Carroll	
Place of birth:	Fermanagh
Date of birth:	30 September 1977
Position:	Goalkeeper
Years at United:	2001–2005
Games played:	72
Goals:	0
Honours:	Premier League (2003); FA Cup (2004)

After enjoying four impressive years between the sticks at Wigan Athletic, Northern Ireland goalkeeper Roy Carroll was snapped up by Manchester United for a fee of £2.5 million in July 2001. Sir Alex Ferguson signed Carroll to help strengthen his senior goalkeeping department, believing him to be one of the most promising keepers in Britain.

While it was a dream move for the twenty-four-year-old Fermanagh native, Carroll faced stiff competition for the number one jersey from none other than French World Cup winner Fabien Barthez. And, during his first full season at the club, Carroll spent much of his time deputising for the Frenchman.

He starred in just seven league games for United that season, but did manage to keep an impressive five clean sheets during that time.

Carroll also made his Champions League debut for United in October 2001, during a 1–1 draw away to French side, Lille.

Roy Carroll.

He was to prove his worth to United in the 2002–03 season when an injury to Barthez, towards the middle of the campaign, gave Carroll an extended run in the first team. He took this opportunity with both hands, and a number of steady displays in goal helped United to clinch the Premier League title that year.

In fact, during the ten league games in which Carroll played, United remained unbeaten.

Despite this, Carroll's first-team opportunities were limited even further after Ferguson signed highly rated American goalkeeper Tim Howard before the start of the 2003–04 season. Carroll made just six league starts during this season, but United again remained unbeaten in each of the games he played.

A major highlight of Carroll's career came when he came on as a substitute for Howard in the 2004 FA Cup final against Millwall. Carroll gave an assured performance between the posts as United ran out comfortable 3–0 winners over their Championship opponents.

Carroll finally became a regular in the United goal for the 2004–05 season, starting in twenty-six Premier League games. Sadly for him, however, his season was blighted by a number of unfortunate errors.

In a league game against Tottenham, he let a speculative lob from midfielder Pedro Mendes, kicked from the halfway line, loop over his head and over the goal line. While he was saved by a poor refereeing decision, which decided against awarding the goal, a second gaffe in a crucial Champions League home game against AC Milan was disastrous.

Carroll let the ball slip out of his grasp in front of Milan striker Hernan Crespo, who scored the goal that knocked United out of the competition.

Carroll did manage to recover from this to play in his second successive FA Cup final in May of that year but, despite keeping a clean sheet during a dour 0–0 draw against Arsenal, he was on the losing side as United lost the resultant penalty shootout.

This proved to be his last game for United, as a month later Carroll signed for West Ham Utd.

During his four seasons at Old Trafford, Roy Carroll played in seventy-two games for Manchester United, keeping an impressive thirty-five clean sheets.

Other Clubs: Ballinamallard Utd, Hull City, Wigan Athletic, West Ham Utd, Rangers, Derby County
International Record: Northern Ireland (still playing)
Caps: 19
Goals: 0

David Healy	
Place of birth:	Down
Date of birth:	5 August 1979
Position:	Striker
Years at United:	1999–2001
Games played:	3
Goals:	0

When prolific young Down striker David Healy signed for Manchester United in August 1999, the Red Devils looked to have a new star in the making.

Playing his football for Down Academy High School, Healy had already proved he could cut it at the top by regularly knocking in goals for Northern Ireland's underage sides.

Healy's biggest problem arriving at Old Trafford was figuring out how to dislodge any of United's excellent international strikers. Andy Cole, Teddy Sheringham, Dwight Yorke and Ole Gunnar Solksjaer had all played their part in leading the club to an historic treble the previous season and were as good as any strikers in the Premier League.

At just twenty years of age, Healy had to make do with playing in United's youth and reserve teams while he waited for the call into the senior squad.

That call duly arrived when he made his debut on 13 October 1999, in a League Cup tie away to Aston Villa. It was the only game which Healy was to feature that season and, in February 2000, he was loaned out to Port Vale to gain first-team experience.

Healy enjoyed his time at Port Vale, playing in sixteen games for the club and scoring three goals. He returned to Man Utd in the summer but was still finding it difficult to get games when the new season came around.

His next outing for United came in a home League Cup tie against Sunderland, when he came on as a ninetieth-minute substitute in a game that went to extra time — and that United eventually lost.

Healy's only league appearance for United came on 28 November 2000, during a 2–0 home win against Ipswich. The young Northern Ireland man came on for Ryan Giggs midway through the second half and almost made an immediate impact when he crashed a shot off the crossbar.

Meanwhile, injuries to some of United's main strikers looked as if it would give Healy an opportunity to show what he could do at Old Trafford. Manager Sir Alex Ferguson had even hinted that he was ready to give Healy a run in the first team.

Instead, he was actually sent out on loan to Preston North End on 29 December 2000, and the move was made permanent five days later in a £1.5 million deal.

Similar to Keith Gillespie before him, Healy's United career was over before it had the chance to get started. And, like Gillespie, Healy has gone on to forge an excellent club career for himself, as well as starring for Northern Ireland.

In fact most of Healy's best football has come on the international stage, where he has scored an incredible thirty-four goals in sixty-four games for his country.

David Healy.

His hat-trick against Spain on 6 September 2006 in Northern Ireland's 3–2 win was the first scored in Belfast since George Best's three-goal salvo against Cyprus in 1971.

Other Clubs: Port Vale, Preston NE, Leeds Utd, Fulham, Sunderland

International Record: Northern Ireland (still playing)

Caps: 69

Goals: 35

John O'Shea	
Place of birth:	Waterford
Date of birth:	30 April 1981
Position:	Defender/Midfielder
Years at United:	1999–present
Games played:	298 (still playing)
Goals:	12
Honours:	Premier League (2003, 2007, 2008);
	FA Cup (2004);
	Carling Cup (2006);
	Champions League (2008)

John O'Shea's affiliation with Manchester United began as a talented teenager, when he made the trip over from his native Waterford to train with the United academy during the summer months.

After completing his schooling, O'Shea signed a professional contract with the club in 1998, whilst still only seventeen years old.

A year later, he made his debut in a Worthington Cup defeat to Aston Villa, but spent most of his first two years playing in Manchester United's reserve team. In January 2000, the nineteen-year-old made the decision to join Second Division side Bournemouth on loan, to gain first-team experience.

O'Shea impressed during his two months at Bournemouth, where he played as a right and left full-back, and even managed to pop up with a rare goal against Millwall. Despite this success, O'Shea's opportunities at United remained limited and he spent more time on loan at Belgian side Royal Antwerp, where he played as a central defender.

O'Shea's breakthrough into the United first team arrived at the beginning of the 2002–03 season, when injuries to some key defenders gave him the opportunity to stake his claim.

He put in some magnificent performances, both in the Premier League and Champions League, and became a fixture in the United team that captured the league title in May 2003. His performances during this season were so good that he was even nominated for the Professional Footballer Association (PFA) Young Player of the Year title.

While he could play in a number of roles, O'Shea was making a name for himself at left-back. Unfortunately for him, he found

it difficult to replicate this form in his second season, as United lost their title to Arsenal. However, he still enjoyed some medal success, playing at left-back at Wembley, as United clinched the FA Cup with victory over Millwall.

The following season, O'Shea's presence in the team was under threat from United's new Argentinian signing Gabriel Heinze, who began to make the left-back position his own, forcing O'Shea to spend more time as a substitute.

As O'Shea was finding it increasingly difficult to hold down a spot in the United defence, manager Sir Alex Ferguson also began to use him as a defensive midfielder. However, injuries to both Heinze and Wes Brown at the start of the 2005–06 season enabled O'Shea to revert back into his defensive role. Then the departure of club captain Roy Keane early in November meant O'Shea was still being used as a midfielder.

As they struggled to overcome Chelsea in the league, a new-look United side still managed to march on to a Carling Cup final date with Wigan. O'Shea started that game in midfield alongside Ryan Giggs and United ran out easy 4–0 winners to capture their first piece of silverware in two years.

In the 2006–07 season, O'Shea found himself playing in a variety of positions including right full-back and even as an emergency goalkeeper. He was forced to don the gloves in a league game against Tottenham after regular goalie Edwin van der Sar picked up an injury and when United had used all three subs.

As makeshift keeper, he even managed to pull off an impressive save from his Irish international team-mate Robbie Keane.

O'Shea further endeared himself to the United fans when he scored a last-minute winner against Liverpool at Anfield in a crucial league game. In all, O'Shea appeared in forty-eight games that season as Sir Alex's men regained the Premier League title they had last won in 2003.

The following season continued in the same vein, with O'Shea mostly being used as a substitute. Starting just seventeen games, he was used from the bench another twenty-one times as United retained their Premier League title after a titanic tussle with Chelsea.

Remarkably, United also had to overcome Chelsea in the Champions League final, but O'Shea was an unused sub on the night.

John O'Shea continues to be an important member of the United squad and is contracted to the club until 2012.

Other Clubs: Bournemouth, Royal Antwerp
International Record: Republic of Ireland (still playing)
Caps: 49
Goals: 1

Liam Miller	
Place of birth:	Cork
Date of birth:	13 February 1981
Position:	Midfielder
Years at United:	2004–2006
Games played:	22
Goals:	2

Corkman Liam Miller burst on to the football stage with some excellent scoring performances for Glasgow Celtic in the Champions League in 2003. Twenty-two-year-old Miller had been at the Scottish giants for the previous six years but really only started to make an impression on their first team during the 2003–04 season.

His swashbuckling displays from midfield had not gone unnoticed and after failing to

Liam Miller.

agree a new contract at Celtic Park, Sir Alex Ferguson moved swiftly so snap up him up for free on a pre-contract agreement in January 2004.

Ferguson was delighted with his acquisition and believed he was signing a young player who could follow in the footsteps of the magnificent Roy Keane.

After finishing that season with Celtic, Miller made his United debut in a challenging Champions League qualifying tie away to Romanian champions Dinamo Bucharest in August 2004. The young Corkman made an immediate impact, coming off the bench to set up United's winning goal after just three minutes on the pitch.

After this excellent start to his Red Devils career, Miller found the going difficult at Old Trafford as he failed to nail down a regular first-team place. He started in just eight league encounters for United during his first season and failed to score in any of those games.

Miller did manage to find the net in a Carling Cup game against Crewe, but it proved to be the only bright spot in an otherwise frustrating season which United finished without winning a trophy.

Miller's second season at Old Trafford was equally disappointing and despite scoring against Barnet in a 4–1 League Cup win, he was eventually loaned out to Championship side Leeds Utd in November 2005. Miller's loan deal was initially for three months, but after impressing at Elland Road, this was extended to the end of the 2005–06 season, where his smart midfield play helped Leeds into the Championship play-off final, where they were beaten 3–0 by Watford.

Miller returned to Manchester Utd having scored one goal during his twenty-eight appearances for Leeds. However, opportunities continued to be limited and he eventually moved to Sunderland for free on 31 August 2006. It proved to be a good move for Miller as he got the chance to team up with his former United team-mate and new Sunderland manager Roy Keane.

Miller left Manchester United after playing just eleven league games in two seasons.

Other Clubs: Celtic, Leeds Utd, Sunderland
International Record: Republic of Ireland (still playing)
Caps: 19
Goals: 1

Darron Gibson	
Place of birth:	Derry
Date of birth:	25 October 1987
Position:	Midfielder
Years at United:	2004–present
Games played:	1 (still playing)
Goals:	0

Derry-born youngster Darron Gibson arrived at Manchester United in 2004 with high hopes of a brilliant future at the famed club.

A powerful and athletic midfielder, Gibson made his full United debut at the tender age of eighteen, in a Carling Cup victory in October 2005, when he was a second-half substitute for Lee Martin in a comfortable 4–1 win for United against ten-man Barnet at Old Trafford.

It was a win that sent United on a long Carling Cup run, which ended in victory over Wigan in the final in February 2006. However, it was also the only senior game which Gibson started in for United that season, as he spent most of his time as an academy and reserve team player.

Gibson became a regular in the United reserve team throughout 2005–06, helping them to win a historic treble, with two goals in nineteen appearances.

In May 2006, Gibson won the prestigious Jimmy Murphy Award as United's Youth Player of the Year and he played regularly for the senior team during their pre-season summer games.

With first team games still likely to be at a premium for young Gibson, United took the decision to send him out on loan to Royal Antwerp in Belgium for the 2006–07 season. Gibson excelled in midfield for the Antwerp side, that looked to regain promotion to the Belgian First Division.

He returned to Manchester in 2007 before being loaned out again to Championship side Wolves, where he spent the majority of the 2007–08 season.

On the international front, Gibson has been involved in a bitter tug-of-war between the Football Association of Ireland (FAI) in the South and Irish Football Association (IFA) in the North. The dispute centres on Gibson's decision to defect from Northern Ireland and play his international football for the Republic. He initially played for the Northern Ireland Under-15 team but is now a regular member of the senior Republic of Ireland squad.

Gibson remains at Manchester United where he will be hoping to nail down a permanent place in the first-team squad.

Other Clubs: Royal Antwerp, Wolves
International Record: Republic of Ireland (still playing)
Caps: 3
Goals: 0

Jonny Evans	
Place of birth:	Belfast
Date of birth:	2 January 1988
Position:	Defender
Years at United:	2006–present
Games played:	4 (still playing)
Goals:	0

Belfast youngster Jonny Evans signed a professional contract with Manchester United in 2006 after progressing through the club's youth academy.

A tall and intelligent centre-back, Evans first started to make his mark on the United reserve team with some very confident performances through the 2005–06 season. He played fourteen games for the reserves that season, scoring two goals, before he was loaned out to Belgian side Royal Antwerp to gain extra experience.

On his return from Antwerp, Evans was snapped up on loan by Sunderland manager, and former United legend, Roy Keane.

Keane immediately used Evans as part of his Sunderland defence which helped the club gain promotion from the Championship back into the Premiership at the end of the 2006–07 season.

Evans returned to United, but was always going to find it difficult to break into a defence that already included the mighty Serb Nemanja Vidic and England internationals Rio Ferdinand and Wes Brown.

Sir Alex did eventually give Evans his Man Utd debut in a League Cup tie at Old Trafford against Championship side Coventry. Unfortunately for Evans, United lost the game 2–0.

Despite this, Ferguson had enough confidence in Evans to include him in the United side for a Champions League home tie against Italian side Roma, which finished in a 1–1 draw. It was the last action Evans was to have at Old Trafford that season as he was again loaned out to Sunderland.

Evans continued to impress for Roy Keane's side and has also excelled for Northern Ireland in any international match he has been called up for.

He is now permanently back at Old Trafford and featured in the centre of United's defence in a big league game against Chelsea, as he took the place of the suspended Vidic. Big things are still expected of Evans at Man Utd.

Other Clubs: Royal Antwerp, Sunderland
International Record: Northern Ireland (still playing)
Caps: 11
Goals: 0

United's Nearly Men

For over the past sixty years, a common dream for thousands of kids across Ireland, who have pulled on a pair of football boots for the first time, has been to play for their beloved Manchester United.

Spurred on by their Old Trafford heroes, hordes of teenagers have made the trip across the Irish Sea in the hope of a glittering Red Devils career. Only a tiny fraction of those ever make the grade, but the very fact that some of the club's greatest players have been Irish keeps this dream alive.

For the teenagers who overcome the initial obstacles of tough training and homesickness, the biggest hurdle remains breaking into the Manchester United first team. Almost every successful Manchester United era has included an Irishman, but for every one who became an Old Trafford hero, another fell just short of the mark.

Many young Irishmen have had to overcome the heartbreak of initial failure at United before enjoying successful club and international football careers. Below is a selection of Irishmen who moved away from Manchester United but still left their mark on the professional game.

Josiah 'Paddy' Sloan	
Place of birth:	Armagh
Date of birth:	30 April 1920
Position:	Right-half/Inside-right
Years at United:	1937–1938

Josiah Sloan left his hometown club Glenavon in 1937 to join Manchester United and even though his football career spanned two decades as he became one of the most travelled footballers ever – he played for twenty different clubs in five countries – he never played in a first-team game at the club.

After just a year at United, Sloan left Old Trafford to join Tranmere Rovers. However, his time at Tranmere was cut short by the outbreak of the Second World War.

During the war, Sloan returned to United and played for the team as a guest in a number of challenge games – he even starred for United in the League Cup North final in May 1945, which they lost 3–2 on aggregate to Bolton Wanderers.

Sloan's appearances for United during this time attracted the attention of Arsenal and when the Football League officially resumed in 1946, Sloan joined the London club.

From there, he moved to Sheffield Utd before travelling to Italy in 1948 to sign up for the mighty AC Milan and became the first Irishman to play in the Italian Serie A. He remained in Italy for three years, where he signed for a host of different clubs, including Torino and Udinese. Sloan ended his Italian adventure when he returned to England in 1951 to sign for Norwich City.

On the international front, Sloan played for the two Ireland teams run by the separate IFA and FAI organisations. Although born in Armagh, Sloan took the opportunity to travel with the FAI's team on a trip to Spain and Portugal in 1946, and even scored the winner in a famous 1–0 win over Spain.

Sloan made three appearances for the IFA team and two for the FAI-run squad, scoring a goal apiece for each of them.

Other Clubs: Glenavon, Tranmere Rovers, Arsenal, Sheffield Utd, AC Milan, Torino, Udinese, Norwich City
International Record: Ireland (IFA & FAI)
Caps: 5
Goals: 2

Eamon Dunphy	
Place of birth:	Dublin
Date of birth:	3 August 1945
Position:	Midfielder
Years at United:	1962–1965

Eamon Dunphy grew up on the streets of 1950s Dublin, watching in awe from a distance as Matt Busby put together his wondrous double-league winning United team.

Twelve-year-old Dunphy was in the crowd the night the Busby Babes waltzed into Dublin for their European Cup date with Shamrock Rovers in 1957, which they duly won 6-0 at Dalymount Park.

Dunphy worked hard at his football and it was to his great delight that scout Billy Behan brought him to Old Trafford in 1962. It was a good time to be Irish at United, as John Giles, Noel Cantwell, Shay Brennan and Tony Dunne all starred in the first team, and a teenage George Best was just about to make his mark.

United won the FA Cup in 1963, with Dunphy looking on from the sidelines. He gained experience in the youth team, but such was the talent in the club at the time, that Dunphy just could not make the breakthrough onto Busby's starting team sheet.

He was a sub on a few occasions as Busby once again transformed United into the top club in England, but with Dunphy's hopes of first-team football at Old Trafford waning, he spent time with York City.

Dunphy eventually left United in 1965 and went on to enjoy a career with London club Millwall in the Second Division. Dunphy spent nine years at Millwall, during which time he was capped twenty-three times for the Republic of Ireland.

Other Clubs: York City, Millwall, Charlton Athletic, Reading
International Record: Republic of Ireland
Caps: 23
Goals: 0

Philip Hughes	
Place of birth:	Manchester
Date of birth:	19 April 1964
Position:	Goalkeeper
Years at United:	1980–1983

Goalkeeper Philip Hughes began his football career with Manchester United when he joined the club as an apprentice in 1980.

He arrived just as United were developing a very good youth team and he played in goal for a side, which also included Norman Whiteside and Mark Hughes, that made it to the final of the 1982 FA Youth Cup, which they lost on aggregate to Watford.

However, with United already blessed with top-class goalkeeping options, such as Gary Bailey, Hughes decided to leave Old Trafford in 1983 to sign professional forms for Leeds Utd. Hughes' two-year stay at Leeds was not happy, though, as he suffered a terrible dislocated shoulder, an injury that reoccurred throughout his career and eventually led to his retirement at the young age of twenty-seven.

Before then, Hughes did manage to have a good career with Bury in the Third Division and was selected to travel with Billy Bingham's Northern Ireland squad to the 1986 World Cup in Mexico when he was the reserve goalkeeper to the legendary Pat Jennings. Hughes was capped three times for his country and would undoubtedly have appeared more for Northern Ireland if his career had not been ended by his persistent shoulder injury.

Other Clubs: Leeds United, Bury
International Record: Northern Ireland
Caps: 3
Goals: 0

Brian Carey	
Place of birth:	Cork
Date of birth:	21 January 1968
Position:	Defender
Years at United:	1989–1993

After impressing Man Utd scouts with some excellent performances at the heart of the Cork City defence, Alex Ferguson was persuaded to bring tall defender Brian Carey to Old Trafford in 1989. He was one of several signings Ferguson made that year in his desperate bid to turn United into genuine league title contenders.

In the four years Carey spent at United, Ferguson achieved his aim of winning the league, but he did it without the Cork defender playing first team football.

During his time at United, Carey also had two spells on loan at Wrexham before being transferred, in November 1993, to Leicester City, where he remained for three years before signing up permanently for Wrexham, a club he would later go on to manage.

Carey was also selected to play for the Republic of Ireland on three occasions, making his debut as a second-half substitute for David O'Leary in an impressive 4–1 win over the USA in 1992.

Other Clubs: Cork City, Wrexham, Leicester
International Record: Republic of Ireland
Caps: 3
Goals: 0

Paul McShane	
Place of birth:	Wicklow
Date of birth:	6 January 1986
Position:	Defender
Years at United:	2002–2006

Defender Paul McShane's determination to play permanent first-team football was ultimately his undoing as a Manchester Utd player. The man from County Wicklow arrived at Old Trafford as a trainee in 2002 and impressed everyone at the club, including Sir Alex Ferguson, with his full-blooded performances.

McShane was part of the talented United youth side that claimed the 2003 FA Youth Cup with victory over Middlesbrough. He was promoted into the first-team squad after this, but United's strong array of defenders meant McShane found it difficult to break into the team.

He moved to Brighton on loan in 2005 and on his return to Old Trafford in 2006, he demanded a transfer from the club and was snapped up by Championship side West Brom.

McShane was a huge success at West Brom and became a popular figure with the fans before deciding, in July 2007, to up sticks to the northeast of England to join Roy Keane's Sunderland revolution.

McShane has also become a regular member of the Republic of Ireland squad, earning a Man of the Match award for an excellent debut performance in a 1–1 draw in an European Championship qualifier with the Czech Republic in Dublin in October 2006.

Other Clubs: St Joseph's Boys, West Brom, Sunderland
International Record: Republic of Ireland
Caps: 11
Goals: 0

All-Star XI

Sam McIlroy

Frank Stapleton

Liam Whelan

George Best

Roy Keane

Norman Whiteside

Johnny Carey

Paul McGrath

Tony Dunne

Denis Irwin

Harry Gregg

Green Devils
All-Star XI

GOALKEEPER

Harry Gregg (1957–1966)

For many of Manchester United's most successful footballers, a cursory glance at their impressive medals tally can be enough to convince of their greatness. However, medals only tell a small part of the story in football, as a player's true worth to a club and his ability as a footballer can be gauged on many different levels.

Derry native Harry Gregg was not only an inspirational figure for Manchester United during the dark days following the Munich Air Disaster in 1958, he was also an exceptional goalkeeper and his strength and skill helped him keep forty-eight clean sheets in goal during his United career.

The only blotch on that career was that Gregg sustained injuries that prevented him from sharing in some of the most glorious moments in Matt Busby's reign. He was cruelly denied an FA Cup winners' medal in 1963 when a shoulder injury prevented him from playing in the final. Likewise, he was injured when United embarked on their successful league winning campaigns in 1965 and 1967.

Nevertheless, with his place in Manchester United's folklore cemented forever, Harry Gregg takes his place in this All-Star Green Devils XI as an immense goalkeeper with few flaws and even fewer equals.

In Reserve: Tommy Breen; Pat Dunne; Roy Carroll

RIGHT FULL-BACK

Denis Irwin (1990–2002)

He may have played for much of his Manchester United career as a left-back, but Denis Irwin takes his place in this Green Devils All-Star XI in his more favoured position on the right side of defence.

A man of few words off the pitch, Irwin did most of his talking on the field of play, giving twelve years of impeccable service to Sir Alex Ferguson's team. A real team player and a true professional, it is hard to highlight just one particular trait from Irwin that shone above everything else he did so well on the pitch.

To say his remarkable consistency was his best strength would be to do a disservice to a guy who was an incredibly good footballer. Irwin had everything you could want from a full-back – good timing in the tackle, brilliant covering for his fellow defenders, good at moving forward with the ball and an excellent crossing ability. To top it all, he had no problem belting or curling a long-range free kick into the top corner of the opponent's net and had a cool head to slot home important penalty kicks when needed.

Everything Irwin did was completed with the maximum of care but with the minimum of fuss and he hardly ever looked out of breath or unduly troubled as he won trophy after trophy at Old Trafford from 1990 until 2002.

He takes his place in the Green Devils' All-Star XI not only as one of Man Utd's best Irish players, but as one of the club's best full-backs of all time.

In Reserve: Shay Brennan; Jimmy Nicholl

LEFT FULL-BACK

Tony Dunne

World-class full-backs can be hard to come by, but it has been Manchester United's great fortune to have been blessed with quite a few, including legendary club stalwart Tony Dunne.

An unsung hero of the great United team of the mid-1960s, Dunne was the dependable and tenacious left full-back in a team that could produce the brilliantly unexpected.

One of Dunne's great attributes was his blinding pace, which enabled him to track and dispossess tricky wingers with the minimum of fuss. Dunne's consistent performances in the United defence allowed his team-mates further up field to attack with abandon as they knew the former Shelbourne man would be there to mop up. Intelligence was also a big part of his make-up as he always seemed to know exactly when to dive in for a tackle and what pass to make.

Dunne's loyalty and commitment to the United cause extended much further than this, however, as he remains one of the club's longest-serving players.

Tony Dunne is a worthy member of the Green Devils All-Star XI and alongside Denis Irwin forms an excellent full-back partnership.

In Reserve: Noel Cantwell

CENTRAL DEFENDER

Paul McGrath (1982–1989)

Paul McGrath's career at Manchester United may not have been laden with medals, but he is still the most naturally gifted defender to have ever come out of Ireland.

As a centre-half, McGrath could read the game so impeccably that he rarely had to break stride to make a clearance or a last-ditch tackle. Worse again for any forward who had the task of trying to evade him, McGrath was also blessed with good pace, could leap like a lion to head clear and would bravely block any shot with whatever part of his anatomy was required.

McGrath was so graceful on the pitch that it was hard to spot any flaws to his game and his modest demeanour belied the true ability he possessed as a footballer and added to his hero status amongst the fans.

McGrath was a stalwart in defence during his seven years at United and his best performances invariably came on the biggest occasions – his Man of the Match display in the 1985 FA Cup final marked him down as one of the greats in the English league at that time.

Although he didn't win a rake of winners' medals with the club, Paul McGrath's place in the Green Devils All Star XI was never in any doubt.

In Reserve: Jackie Blanchflower

CENTRAL DEFENDER

Johnny Carey (1936–1953)

As the first Irishman to captain United to major trophy success, Johnny Carey was also one of the country's first real soccer stars.

A player of unbelievable versatility, Carey could play in practically every position on the pitch, but he takes his place alongside Paul McGrath in the centre of the Green Devils' defence.

Although he lost a huge part of his career to the Second World War, his crucial leadership qualities were always going to be in demand when the Football League resumed and United's new manager Matt Busby had no hesitation in making Carey the team captain.

One of Carey's best strengths as a defender was his uncanny ability to read the game. What he lacked in pace, he made up for in cunning, which enabled him to make clean tackles quickly that would set United on the counter-attack.

Carey was also an incredibly fair and honest player, who deserved his moment of glory in 1948 when he captained United to win the FA Cup.

He was also an extremely consistent performer during his time with United, when they finished runners-up in the league four times in five years before finally leading United to their first league title under Matt Busby in 1953.

Alongside Paul McGrath, Carey forms an inspirational central defensive partnership that could grace any great Man Utd team.

In Reserve: Kevin Moran

CENTRAL MIDFIELD

Roy Keane (1993–2005)

Has there ever been a more tough, committed, talented and downright courageous player for Manchester United than Roy Keane?

As the club's most successful captain, Keane goes down in history as not just one of Ireland's best players, but as one of the best midfielders the English game has ever seen.

The complete box-to-box midfielder, there wasn't a blade of grass on the Old Trafford pitch that didn't become acquainted with the studs of Keane's boots as he, playing as if he would prefer to lose a leg than lose a football match, drove United on to one great success after another.

What Keane also possessed was a vital attribute reserved only for the very best players – the ability to raise his game for the big occasion. In a dour FA Cup final with bitter rivals Liverpool in 1996, Keane was head and shoulders above everyone on the Wembley pitch. Eric Cantona may have gained the plaudits for the magnificent goal that won the game, but Keane's vital influence was rewarded with the Man of the Match award.

Leading by example, Keane was never found wanting on a football pitch and his sheer honesty of effort helped improve the game of each United player around him. Keane garnered huge respect from his team-mates, who always knew their captain would be on their back if they shirked their responsibilities.

The only misfortune for Keane during his illustrious United career was his noted absence from the team's 1999 Champions League final victory. Football can be a cruel game and Keane learned this to his cost that year, when a yellow card picked up against Juventus in the semi-final denied him his chance of leading United to European glory.

Yet without Keane, United would never have made it to the Champions League final that year. It was only through his sheer inability to accept defeat that the Red Devils pulled back a two-goal deficit to beat Juventus in Turin after United had endured a horrific start to that game.

Roy Keane's true worth to Manchester United over the twelve years he was at the club could never be in doubt and he takes his place as the central force of the Green Devils team.

In Reserve: John Giles

CENTRAL MIDFIELD

Norman Whiteside (1978–1989)

Big, strong and up for anything – Norman Whiteside may not have played for all of his Manchester United career as a central midfielder but there's no doubt he possessed the ability to shine there.

Bursting on to the world stage at just seventeen, Whiteside was a powerhouse player with an exquisite touch on the ball and his ability to turn a game on its head with a sublime pass, cross or goal made him an instant hit with the Man Utd fans.

A great header of the ball and an all-action tough tackler, Whiteside had a bit of everything in his arsenal, including the ability to score vital goals on the big occasion. The highlight of his United career, and a moment which best summed up the north Belfast man's unique ability, was his exquisite winner in the 1985 FA Cup final with Everton.

He will always be remembered as one of United's most talented players and a true character. Playing alongside Roy Keane, Whiteside would have given United a formidable partnership in midfield.

In Reserve: David McCreery; Gerry Daly

RIGHT-WING

George Best (1962–1974)

Is there really any need to name or explain the reason for selecting George Best on the right wing of the Green Devils' XI team?

The wondrous Best, the most talented Irishman to have ever set foot on to a football pitch, takes his place as the most dazzling star amongst a team of truly excellent United servants.

With the ability to ghost past players with a dazzling array of silky skills and pace, Best's arrival in Manchester in the mid-1960s was a godsend for manager Matt Busby, who had watched helplessly as the phenomenally talented Busby Babes he had nurtured during the 1950s were wiped out by the tragic events of the Munich Air Disaster. Despite Busby's determination, it was always going to be difficult to replicate that team again – until George Best came along. The free-spirited Best encapsulated the vision Busby had for the way the game should be played.

Playing predominantly on the right-wing, Best was as comfortable with the ball on either foot as he continuously made a mockery of defenders' flailing efforts to stop him.

By the tender age of twenty-two, Best had conquered Europe with United, by winning the European Cup and being named the continent's Player of the Year in 1968.

With the world at his feet, Best could have remained the game's greatest player for at least another decade, but his flamboyant lifestyle led him down another path. Though, for the remaining six years at United, he continued to be the club's best player and had achieved more by the age of twenty-seven than most players dream of.

But one thing is certain. His standing as the most naturally gifted player to have ever donned the red shirt of Manchester United remains firmly intact.

In Reserve: Keith Gillespie

LEFT-WING

Liam Whelan (1953–1958)

It is difficult to know exactly where to place Liam Whelan in the Green Devils XI, bearing in mind he played as an inside-forward during a time when football used a much different system to the modern 4-4-2 formation.

But given his incredible scoring ratio during his brief United career and the impact he made on the legendary Busby Babes, Whelan was always likely to be accommodated in some attacking part of the team.

Whether the left-wing position would have suited Whelan best may be debatable, but the guile and skill he showed while playing for the double league winning team of the 1950s ensures he wouldn't have been out of place on any part of the pitch.

Shorn of genuine pace, Whelan made up for it with a lightning brain which left many defenders trailing in his wake.

A quiet spoken man away from the pitch, Whelan was another player who let his football do his talking and he possessed a lethal streak when in front of goal and rarely missed when presented with an opportunity to score but he also had the capability of producing goals on his own. One major trick Whelan used to great effect was the dummy. He had an uncanny ability to feint going one way with the ball before taking off past bewildered defenders in the other direction and could dribble as good as any player in the game.

An example of his incredible ability to ghost past players came in a European Cup quarter-final clash away to Athletico Bilbao in 1956. With just minutes remaining on the clock, Whelan scored an audacious goal any player from Pele to Maradona would have been proud of.

Liam Whelan was only twenty-two when he died in the Munich Air Disaster in February 1958. The very fact that he had already won two league titles and scored numerous important goals makes him a huge addition to this Green Devils XI.

In Reserve: Mickey Hamill; John Peden

FORWARD

Frank Stapleton (1981–1987)

Dubliner Frank Stapleton is by far the best Irish centre-forward to have ever donned the red shirt of Man Utd.

Brave, strong and committed, Stapleton was an extremely unselfish front man for the club, doing as much to help bring team-mates into the game as he did in finding the back of the net himself. He possessed an incredible aerial ability and did much of his best work with his head.

Stapleton could inspire others around him to perform and he was part of an extremely talented United squad that should have won more than just the two FA Cups they achieved under Ron Atkinson's reign in the 1980s.

While he was a complete all-round performer, Stapleton was still the man United looked to for goals and he was the team's leading goalscorer for the majority of the six seasons he played for the club. He had excellent close control which always enabled him to retain possession up the field and sustain attacks for his team. Stapleton was worth his weight in gold at United, combining his skills and industry to great effect.

His greatest strength was his ability work with others so in a team as good as this Green Devils XI he would have flourished. With Best, Whelan, Whiteside and McIlroy all adding their own offensive style to the mix, Stapleton would surely have found himself amongst the goals on a regular basis.

In Reserve: David Healy; Don Givens

FORWARD

Sam McIlroy (1971–1981)

Few players made as much an impact on Manchester United in the decade following Matt Busby's departure as manager than the tenacious Sammy McIlroy.

One of Busby's last duties as manager was to bring McIlroy to the club and, as with almost everything the great man did, it proved to be an inspired piece of business.

Starting life as a striker for United, McIlory scored on his debut in the Manchester derby, but it wasn't until his later career in the United midfield when the Belfast man really made his name.

What he may have lacked in overall strength as a footballer, McIlroy made up for with intuitive natural ability which helped him score and create many important goals for the club. He had tremendously quick feet and beautiful balance that enabled him to evade tackles and set his team on attack.

He was another man for the big occasion, as he evidently showed with his brilliant goal at Wembley against Arsenal in the 1979 FA Cup final.

Talent was only one part of the McIlroy make-up, however, as he also possessed an excellent work-rate and huge heart for the battle – traits that helped him survive a ropey period at United during the mid-1970s when the club slumped out of the First Division.

Playing with huge pride in the red shirt, McIlroy symbolised this reinvigorated Man United and he helped the club to two FA Cup finals in 1976 and 1977, the latter of which was a glorious win over Liverpool.

Although operating mostly on the left for United during the late 1970s, McIlroy partners Frank Stapleton in this Green Devils' frontline full of grit, determination and no lack of goal scoring talent.

In Reserve: Harry Baird

Statistics

NEWTON HEATH IN FIRST DIVISION

SEASON 1892–93

	P	W	D	L	F	A	PTS
Sunderland	30	22	4	4	100	36	48
Preston NE	30	17	3	10	57	39	37
Everton	30	16	4	10	74	51	36
Aston Villa	30	16	3	11	73	62	35
Bolton Wanderers	30	13	6	11	56	55	32
Burnley	30	13	4	13	51	44	30
Stoke City	30	12	5	13	58	48	29
West Brom	30	12	5	13	58	69	29
Blackburn	30	8	13	9	47	53	29
Nottingham Forest	30	10	8	12	48	52	28
Wolves	30	12	4	14	47	68	28
Sheffield Wed	30	12	3	15	55	65	27
Derby County	30	9	9	12	52	64	27
Nottingham County	30	10	4	16	53	61	24
Accrington Stanley	30	6	11	13	57	81	23
NEWTON HEATH	**30**	**6**	**6**	**18**	**50**	**85**	**18**

SEASON 1893–94

	P	W	D	L	F	A	PTS
Aston Villa	30	19	6	5	84	42	44
Sunderland	30	17	4	9	72	44	38
Derby County	30	16	4	10	73	62	36
Blackburn Rovers	30	16	2	12	69	53	34
Burnley	30	15	4	11	61	51	34
Everton	30	15	3	12	90	57	33
Nottingham Forest	30	14	4	12	57	48	32
West Brom	30	14	4	12	66	59	32
Wolves	30	14	3	13	52	63	31
Sheffield Utd	30	13	5	12	47	61	31
Stoke City	30	13	3	14	65	79	29
Sheffield Wed	30	9	8	13	48	57	26
Bolton Wanderers	30	10	4	16	38	52	24
Preston NE	30	10	3	17	44	56	23
Darwen	30	7	5	18	37	83	19
NEWTON HEATH	**30**	**6**	**2**	**22**	**36**	**72**	**14**

YEARS MANCHESTER UNITED CROWNED CHAMPIONS:

SEASON 1907–08

	P	W	D	L	F	A	PTS
Manchester United	**38**	**23**	**6**	**9**	**81**	**49**	**52**
Aston Villa	38	16	11	11	77	59	43
Manchester City	38	16	11	11	62	54	43
Newcastle Utd	38	15	12	11	65	54	42
Sheffield Wed	38	19	4	15	73	64	42
Middlesbrough	38	17	7	14	54	45	41
Bury	38	14	11	13	58	61	39
Liverpool	38	16	6	16	58	51	38
Nottingham Forest	38	13	11	14	59	62	37
Bristol City	38	12	12	14	58	61	36
Everton	38	15	6	17	58	64	36
Preston NE	38	12	12	14	47	53	36
Chelsea	38	14	8	16	53	62	36
Blackburn Rovers	38	12	12	14	51	63	36
Arsenal	38	12	12	14	51	63	36
Sunderland	38	16	3	19	78	75	35
Sheffield Utd	38	12	11	15	52	58	35
Nottingham County	38	13	8	17	39	51	34
Bolton Wanderers	38	14	5	19	52	58	33
Birmingham City	38	9	12	17	40	60	30

SEASON 1910–11

	P	W	D	L	F	A	PTS
Manchester United	**38**	**22**	**8**	**8**	**72**	**40**	**52**
Aston Villa	38	22	7	9	73	41	51
Sunderland	38	15	15	8	67	48	45
Everton	38	20	5	13	50	33	45
Bradford City	38	20	5	13	51	42	45
Sheffield Wed	38	17	8	13	47	48	42
Oldham Athletic	38	16	9	13	44	41	41
Newcastle Utd	38	15	10	13	61	43	40
Sheffield Utd	38	15	8	15	49	43	38
Arsenal	38	13	12	13	41	49	38
Notts County	38	14	10	14	37	45	38
Blackburn Rovers	38	13	11	11	62	54	37

	P	W	D	L	F	A	PTS
Liverpool	38	15	7	16	53	53	37
Preston NE	38	12	11	15	40	49	35
Tottenham Hotspur	38	13	6	19	52	63	32
Middlesbrough	38	11	10	17	49	63	32
Manchester City	38	9	13	16	43	58	31
Bury	38	9	11	18	43	71	29
Bristol City	38	11	5	22	43	66	27
Nottingham Forest	38	9	7	22	45	75	25

SEASON 1951–52

	P	W	D	L	F	A	PTS
Manchester United	**42**	**23**	**11**	**8**	**95**	**52**	**57**
Tottenham Hotspur	42	22	9	11	76	51	53
Arsenal	42	21	11	10	70	51	53
Portsmouth	42	20	8	14	68	58	48
Bolton Wanderers	42	19	10	13	65	61	47
Aston Villa	42	19	9	14	79	70	47
Preston NE	42	17	12	13	74	54	46
Newcastle Utd	42	18	9	15	98	73	45
Blackpool	42	18	9	15	64	64	45
Charlton Athletic	42	17	10	15	68	64	44
Liverpool	42	12	19	11	57	61	43
Sunderland	42	15	12	15	70	61	42
West Brom	42	14	13	15	64	67	41
Burnley	42	15	10	17	56	63	40
Manchester City	42	13	13	16	58	61	39
Wolves	42	12	14	16	73	73	38
Derby County	42	15	7	20	63	80	37
Middlesbrough	42	15	6	21	64	88	36
Chelsea	42	14	8	21	52	72	36
Stoke City	42	12	7	23	49	88	31
Huddersfield Town	42	10	8	24	49	82	28
Fulham	42	8	11	23	58	77	27

SEASON 1955–56

	P	W	D	L	F	A	PTS
Manchester United	**42**	**25**	**10**	**7**	**83**	**51**	**60**
Blackpool	42	20	9	13	86	52	49

	P	W	D	L	F	A	PTS
Wolves	42	20	9	13	89	65	49
Manchester City	42	18	10	14	82	69	46
Arsenal	42	18	10	14	60	61	46
Birmingham City	42	18	9	15	75	58	45
Burnley	42	18	8	16	64	54	44
Bolton Wanderers	42	18	7	17	71	58	43
Sunderland	42	17	9	16	80	95	43
Luton Town	42	17	8	17	66	64	42
Newcastle Utd	42	17	7	18	85	70	41
Portsmouth	42	16	9	17	78	85	41
West Brom	42	18	5	19	58	70	41
Charlton Athletic	42	17	6	19	75	81	40
Everton	42	15	10	17	55	69	40
Chelsea	42	14	11	17	64	77	39
Cardiff City	42	15	9	18	55	69	39
Tottenham Hotspur	42	15	7	20	51	61	37
Preston NE	42	14	8	20	73	72	36
Aston Villa	42	11	13	18	52	69	35
Huddersfield Town	42	14	7	21	54	83	35
Sheffield Utd	42	12	9	21	63	77	33

SEASON 1956–57

	P	W	D	L	F	A	PTS
Manchester United	**42**	**28**	**8**	**6**	**103**	**54**	**64**
Tottenham Hotspur	42	22	12	8	104	56	56
Preston NE	42	23	10	9	84	56	56
Blackpool	42	22	9	11	93	65	53
Arsenal	42	21	8	13	85	69	52
Wolves	42	20	8	14	94	70	48
Burnley	42	18	10	14	56	50	46
Leeds Utd	42	15	14	13	72	63	44
Bolton Wanderers	42	16	12	14	65	65	44
Aston Villa	42	14	15	13	65	55	43
West Brom	42	14	14	14	59	61	42
Birmingham City	42	15	9	18	69	69	39
Chelsea	42	13	13	6	73	73	39
Sheffield Wed	42	16	6	20	82	88	38
Everton	42	14	10	18	61	79	38
Luton Town	42	14	9	19	58	76	37

	P	W	D	L	F	A	PTS
Newcastle Utd	42	14	8	20	67	97	36
Manchester City	42	13	9	20	78	88	35
Portsmouth	42	10	13	19	62	92	33
Sunderland	42	12	8	22	67	88	32
Cardiff City	42	10	9	23	53	88	29
Charlton Athletic	42	9	4	29	42	110	22

SEASON 1964–65

	P	W	D	L	F	A	PTS
Manchester United	**42**	**26**	**9**	**7**	**89**	**39**	**61**
Leeds Utd	42	26	9	7	83	52	61
Chelsea	42	24	8	10	89	54	56
Everton	42	17	15	10	69	60	49
Nottingham Forest	42	17	13	12	71	67	47
Tottenham Hotspur	42	19	7	16	87	71	45
Liverpool	42	17	10	15	67	73	44
Sheffield Wed	42	16	11	15	57	55	43
West Ham Utd	42	19	4	19	82	71	42
Blackburn Rovers	42	16	10	16	83	79	42
Stoke City	42	16	10	16	67	66	42
Burnley	42	16	10	16	70	70	42
Arsenal	42	17	7	18	69	75	41
West Brom	42	13	13	16	70	65	39
Sunderland	42	14	9	19	64	74	37
Aston Villa	42	16	5	21	57	82	37
Blackpool	42	12	11	19	67	78	35
Leicester City	42	11	13	18	69	85	35
Sheffield Utd	42	12	11	19	50	64	35
Fulham	42	11	12	19	60	78	33
Wolves	42	13	4	25	59	89	30
Birmingham City	42	8	11	23	64	96	27

SEASON 1966–67

	P	W	D	L	F	A	PTS
Manchester United	**42**	**24**	**12**	**6**	**84**	**45**	**60**
Nottingham Forest	42	23	10	9	64	41	56
Tottenham Hotspur	42	24	8	10	71	48	56
Leeds Utd	42	22	11	9	62	42	55

	P	W	D	L	F	A	PTS
Liverpool	42	19	13	10	64	47	51
Everton	42	19	10	13	65	46	48
Arsenal	42	16	14	12	58	47	46
Leicester City	42	18	8	16	78	71	44
Chelsea	42	15	14	13	67	62	44
Sheffield Utd	42	16	10	16	52	59	42
Sheffield Wed	42	14	13	15	56	47	41
Stoke City	42	17	7	18	63	58	41
West Brom	42	16	7	19	77	73	39
Burnley	42	15	9	18	66	76	39
Manchester City	42	12	15	15	43	52	39
West Ham Utd	42	14	8	20	80	84	36
Sunderland	42	14	8	20	58	72	36
Fulham	42	11	12	19	71	84	34
Southampton	42	14	6	22	74	92	34
Newcastle Utd	42	12	9	21	39	81	33
Aston Villa	42	11	7	24	54	85	29
Blackpool	42	6	9	27	41	76	21

SEASON 1992–93

	P	W	D	L	F	A	PTS
Manchester United	**42**	**24**	**12**	**6**	**67**	**31**	**84**
Aston Villa	42	21	11	10	57	40	74
Norwich City	42	21	9	12	61	65	72
Blackburn Rovers	42	20	11	11	68	46	71
Queens Park Rangers	42	17	12	13	63	55	63
Liverpool	42	16	11	15	62	55	59
Sheffield Wed	42	15	14	13	55	51	59
Tottenham Hotspur	42	16	11	15	60	66	59
Manchester City	42	15	12	15	56	51	57
Arsenal	42	15	11	16	40	38	56
Chelsea	42	14	14	14	51	54	56
Wimbledon	42	14	12	16	56	55	54
Everton	42	15	8	19	53	55	53
Sheffield Utd	42	14	10	18	54	53	52
Coventry City	42	13	13	16	52	57	52
Ipswich Town	42	12	16	14	50	55	52
Leeds Utd	42	12	15	15	57	62	51
Southampton	42	13	11	18	54	61	50

	P	W	D	L	F	A	PTS
Oldham Athletic	42	13	10	19	63	74	49
Crystal Palace	42	11	16	15	48	61	49
Middlesbrough	42	11	11	20	54	75	44
Nottingham Forest	42	10	10	22	41	62	40

SEASON 1993–94

	P	W	D	L	F	A	PTS
Manchester United	**42**	**27**	**11**	**4**	**80**	**38**	**92**
Blackburn Rovers	42	25	9	8	63	36	84
Newcastle Utd	42	23	8	11	82	41	77
Arsenal	42	18	17	7	53	28	71
Leeds Utd	42	18	16	8	65	39	70
Wimbledon	42	18	11	13	56	53	65
Sheffield Wed	42	16	16	10	76	54	64
Liverpool	42	17	9	16	59	55	60
Queens Park Rangers	42	16	12	14	62	61	60
Aston Villa	42	15	12	15	46	50	57
Coventry City	42	14	14	14	43	45	56
Norwich City	42	12	17	13	65	61	53
West Ham Utd	42	13	13	16	47	58	52
Chelsea	42	13	12	17	49	53	51
Tottenham Hotspur	42	11	12	19	54	59	45
Manchester City	42	9	18	15	38	49	45
Everton	42	12	8	22	42	63	44
Southampton	42	12	7	23	49	66	43
Ipswich Town	42	9	16	17	35	58	43
Sheffield Utd	42	8	18	16	42	60	42
Oldham Athletic	42	9	13	20	42	68	40
Swindon Town	42	5	15	22	47	100	30

SEASON 1995–96

	P	W	D	L	F	A	PTS
Manchester United	**38**	**25**	**7**	**6**	**73**	**35**	**82**
Newcastle Utd	38	24	6	8	66	37	78
Liverpool	38	20	11	7	70	34	71
Aston Villa	38	18	9	11	52	35	63
Arsenal	38	17	12	9	49	32	63
Everton	38	17	10	11	64	44	61

	P	W	D	L	F	A	PTS
Blackburn Rovers	38	18	7	13	61	47	61
Tottenham Hotspur	38	16	13	9	50	38	61
Nottingham Forest	38	15	13	10	50	54	58
West Ham Utd	38	14	9	15	43	52	51
Chelsea	38	12	14	12	46	44	50
Middlesbrough	38	11	10	17	35	50	43
Leeds Utd	38	12	7	19	40	57	43
Wimbledon	38	10	11	17	55	70	41
Sheffield Wed	38	10	10	18	48	61	40
Coventry City	38	8	14	16	42	60	38
Southampton	38	9	11	18	34	52	38
Manchester City	38	9	11	18	34	59	38
Queens Park Rangers	38	9	6	23	38	57	33
Bolton Wanderers	38	8	5	25	39	71	29

SEASON 1996–97

	P	W	D	L	F	A	PTS
Manchester United	**38**	**21**	**12**	**5**	**76**	**44**	**75**
Newcastle Utd	38	19	11	8	73	40	68
Arsenal	38	19	11	8	62	32	68
Liverpool	38	19	11	8	62	37	68
Aston Villa	38	17	10	11	47	34	61
Chelsea	38	16	11	11	58	55	59
Sheffield Wed	38	14	15	9	50	51	57
Wimbledon	38	15	11	12	49	46	56
Leicester City	38	12	11	15	46	54	47
Tottenham Hotspur	38	13	7	18	44	51	46
Leeds Utd	38	11	13	14	28	38	46
Derby County	38	11	13	14	45	58	46
Blackburn Rovers	38	9	15	14	42	43	42
West Ham Utd	38	10	12	16	39	48	42
Everton	38	10	12	16	44	57	42
Southampton	38	10	11	17	50	56	41
Coventry City	38	9	14	15	38	54	41
Sunderland	38	10	10	18	35	53	40
Middlesbrough	38	10	12	16	51	60	39
Nottingham Forest	38	6	16	16	31	59	34

SEASON 1998–99

	P	W	D	L	F	A	PTS
Manchester United	**38**	**22**	**13**	**3**	**80**	**37**	**79**
Arsenal	38	22	12	4	59	17	78
Chelsea	38	20	15	3	57	30	75
Leeds Utd	38	18	13	7	62	34	67
West Ham Utd	38	16	8	11	46	53	56
Aston Villa	38	15	10	13	51	46	55
Liverpool	38	15	9	14	68	49	54
Derby County	38	13	13	12	40	45	52
Middlesbrough	38	12	15	11	48	54	51
Leicester City	38	12	13	13	40	46	49
Tottenham Hotspur	38	11	14	13	47	50	47
Sheffield Wed	38	13	7	18	31	36	46
Newcastle Utd	38	11	13	14	48	54	46
Everton	38	11	10	17	42	47	43
Coventry City	38	11	9	18	39	51	42
Wimbledon	38	10	12	16	40	63	42
Southampton	38	11	8	19	37	64	41
Charlton Athletic	38	8	12	18	41	56	36
Blackburn Rovers	38	7	14	17	38	52	35
Nottingham Forest	38	7	9	22	31	65	30

SEASON 1999–2000

	P	W	D	L	F	A	PTS
Manchester United	**38**	**28**	**7**	**3**	**97**	**45**	**91**
Arsenal	38	22	7	9	73	43	73
Leeds Utd	38	21	6	11	58	43	69
Liverpool	38	19	10	9	51	30	67
Chelsea	38	18	11	9	53	34	65
Aston Villa	38	15	13	10	46	35	58
Sunderland	38	16	19	12	57	56	57
Leicester City	38	16	7	15	55	55	55
West Ham Utd	38	15	10	13	52	55	55
Tottenham Hotspur	38	15	8	15	57	49	53
Newcastle Utd	38	14	10	14	63	54	52
Middlesbrough	38	14	10	14	46	52	52
Everton	38	12	14	12	59	49	50
Coventry City	38	12	8	18	47	54	44

	P	W	D	L	F	A	PTS
Southampton	38	12	8	18	45	52	44
Derby County	38	9	11	18	44	57	38
Bradford City	38	9	9	20	38	68	36
Wimbledon	38	7	12	19	46	74	33
Sheffield Wed	38	8	7	23	38	70	31
Watford	38	6	6	26	35	77	24

SEASON 2000–2001

	P	W	D	L	F	A	PTS
Manchester United	**38**	**24**	**8**	**6**	**79**	**31**	**80**
Arsenal	38	20	10	8	53	38	70
Liverpool	38	20	9	9	71	39	69
Leeds Utd	38	20	8	10	64	43	68
Ipswich Town	38	20	6	12	57	42	66
Chelsea	38	17	10	11	68	43	61
Sunderland	38	15	12	11	46	41	57
Aston Villa	38	13	15	10	46	43	54
Charlton Athletic	38	14	10	14	50	57	52
Southampton	38	14	10	14	40	48	52
Newcastle Utd	38	14	9	15	44	50	51
Tottenham Hotspur	38	13	10	15	47	54	49
Leicester City	38	14	6	18	39	51	48
Middlesbrough	38	9	15	14	44	44	42
West Ham Utd	38	10	12	16	45	50	42
Everton	38	11	9	18	45	59	42
Derby County	38	10	12	16	37	59	42
Manchester City	38	8	10	20	41	65	34
Coventry City	38	8	10	20	36	63	34
Bradford City	38	5	11	22	30	70	26

SEASON 2002–2003

	P	W	D	L	F	A	PTS
Manchester United	**38**	**25**	**8**	**5**	**74**	**34**	**83**
Arsenal	38	23	9	6	85	42	78
Newcastle Utd	38	21	6	11	63	48	69
Chelsea	38	19	10	9	68	38	67
Liverpool	38	18	10	10	61	41	64
Blackburn Rovers	38	16	12	10	52	43	60

	P	W	D	L	F	A	PTS
Everton	38	17	8	13	48	49	59
Southampton	38	13	13	12	43	46	52
Manchester City	38	15	6	17	47	54	51
Tottenham Hotspur	38	14	8	16	51	62	50
Middlesbrough	38	13	10	15	48	44	49
Charlton Athletic	38	14	7	17	45	56	49
Birmingham City	38	13	9	16	41	49	48
Fulham	38	13	9	16	41	50	48
Leeds Utd	38	14	5	19	58	57	47
Bolton Wanderers	38	10	14	14	41	51	44
West Ham Utd	38	10	12	16	42	59	42
West Brom	38	6	8	24	29	65	26
Sunderland	38	4	7	27	21	65	19

SEASON 2006–2007

	P	W	D	L	F	A	PTS
Manchester United	**38**	**28**	**5**	**5**	**83**	**27**	**89**
Chelsea	38	24	11	3	64	24	83
Liverpool	38	20	8	10	57	26	68
Arsenal	38	19	11	8	63	35	68
Tottenham Hotspur	38	17	9	12	57	54	60
Everton	38	15	13	10	52	36	58
Bolton Wanderers	38	16	8	14	47	52	56
Reading	38	16	7	15	52	47	55
Portsmouth	38	14	12	12	45	42	54
Blackburn Rovers	38	15	7	16	52	54	52
Aston Villa	38	11	17	10	43	41	50
Middlesbrough	38	12	10	16	44	49	46
Newcastle Utd	38	11	10	17	38	47	43
Manchester City	38	11	9	18	29	44	42
West Ham Utd	38	12	5	21	35	59	41
Fulham	38	8	15	15	38	6	39
Wigan Athletic	38	10	8	20	37	59	38
Sheffield Utd	38	10	8	20	32	55	38
Charlton Athletic	38	8	10	20	34	60	34
Watford	38	5	13	20	29	59	28

SEASON 2007–2008

	P	W	D	L	F	A	PTS
Manchester United	**38**	**27**	**6**	**5**	**80**	**21**	**87**
Chelsea	38	25	10	3	65	26	85
Arsenal	38	24	11	3	74	31	83
Liverpool	38	21	13	4	67	28	76
Everton	38	19	8	11	55	33	65
Aston Villa	38	16	12	10	71	51	60
Blackburn Rovers	38	15	13	1	50	48	58
Portsmouth	38	16	9	13	48	40	57
Manchester City	38	15	10	13	45	53	55
West Ham Utd	38	13	10	15	42	50	49
Tottenham Hotspur	38	11	13	14	66	61	44
Newcastle Utd	38	11	10	17	45	65	43
Middlesbrough	38	10	12	16	43	53	43
Wigan Athletic	38	10	10	18	34	51	40
Sunderland	38	11	6	21	36	59	39
Bolton Wanderers	38	9	10	19	36	54	37
Fulham	38	8	12	18	38	60	36
Reading	38	10	6	22	41	26	36
Birmingham City	38	8	11	19	46	62	35
Derby County	38	1	8	29	20	89	11

MANCHESTER UNITED FA CUP FINAL WINS

1909
Manchester United 1–0 Bristol City (Turnbull)

1948
Manchester United 4–2 Blackpool (Rowley (2), Anderson, Pearson)

1963
Manchester United 3–1 Leicester City (Herd (2), Law)

1977
Manchester United 2–1 Liverpool (Greenhoff, Pearson)

1983
Manchester United 2–2 Brighton (Stapleton, Wilkins)
Replay: Manchester United 4–0 Brighton (Robson (2), Muhren, Whiteside)

1985
Manchester United 1–0 Everton (Whiteside)

1990
Manchester United 3–3 Crystal Palace (Hughes (2), Robson)
Replay: Manchester United 1–0 Crystal Palace (Martin)

1994
Manchester United 4–0 Chelsea (Cantona (2), Hughes, McClair)

1996
Manchester United 1–0 Liverpool (Cantona)

1999
Manchester United 2–0 Newcastle (Scholes, Sheringham)

2004
Manchester United 3–0 Millwall (van Nistelroy (2), Ronaldo)

LEAGUE CUP FINAL WINS

1992

Manchester United 1–0 Nottingham Forest (McClair)

2006

Manchester United 4–0 Wigan Athletic (Rooney (2), Ronaldo, Saha)

EUROPEAN CUP FINAL WINS

1968

Manchester United 4–1 Benfica (Charlton (2), Best, Kidd)

1999

Manchester United 2–1 Bayern Munich (Sheringham, Solksjaer)

2008

Manchester United 1–1 Chelsea (Ronaldo)

United won 5–4 on penalties

EUROPEAN CUP WINNERS CUP FINAL WINS

1991

Manchester United 2–1 Barcelona (Hughes (2))

EUROPEAN SUPER CUP FINAL WINS

1991

Manchester United 1–0 Red Star Belgrade (McClair)

INTER-CONTINENTAL CUP FINAL WINS

1999

Manchester United 1–0 Palmeiras (Keane)

Photographic Permissions

The author and publisher would like to thank the following for allowing the use of their copyrighted material in *Green Devils*.

Inpho Photography: Inpho/Donal Farmer: ii; 196 • Inpho/Allsport: 60; 126–127; 176; 187; 188; 193; 201 • Inpho/Getty Images: 168; 191; 194–195; 206; 208

Colorsport: 10; 14; 16; 17; 20; 21; 24; 26; 28; 30; 32; 34; 38; 39; 42; 48; 49; 50; 52; 53; 54; 57; 64; 67; 68–69; 77; 78; 79; 80; 81; 82; 83; 86; 87; 89; 90; 92; 93; 95; 101; 102; 105; 109; 113; 116; 123; 124; 125; 129; 131; 133; 136; 138; 144; 155; 157; 158; 159; 172; 174; 189 • Colorsport/Andrew Cowie: 57; 110; 115; 117; 120; 122; 135; 141; 143; 149; 150; 151; 153; 173; 182; 184; 198; 204 • Colorsport/Stuart MacFarlane: 175 • Colorsport/Kieran Galvin: 177

Getty Images: Bob Thomas/Popperfoto/Getty Images: 4; 6; 15 • Popperfoto/Getty Images: 41; 103; 165 • Central Press/Getty Images: 65 • Wesley/Getty Images: 66 • Bob Thomas/Getty Images: 146

Eddie Gibbons: 167

The author and publisher have endeavoured to contact all copyright holders. If any images used in this book have been reproduced without permission, we would like to rectify this in future editions and encourage owners of copyright not acknowledged to contact us.